THE WALTER LYNWOOD FLEMING LECTURES IN SOUTHERN HISTORY

LOUISIANA STATE UNIVERSITY

NOTHING
BUT FREEDOM

NOTHING
BUT
FREEDOM

EMANCIPATION AND
ITS LEGACY

Eric Foner

LOUISIANA STATE UNIVERSITY PRESS

BATON ROUGE AND LONDON

Designer: Barbara Werden
Typeface: Linotron Trump
Typesetter: G&S Typesetters, Inc.
Printer: Thomson-Shore, Inc.

LIBRARY OF CONGRESS CATALOGING IN PUBLICATION DATA

Foner, Eric.
  Nothing but freedom.

  (The Walter Lynwood Fleming lectures in southern
history)
  Includes bibliographical references and index.
    1. Slavery—Emancipation.   2. Slavery in the
United States—Emancipation.   3. Reconstruction.
4. Liberty.   5. Labor and laboring classes—United
States—History—19th century.   I. Title.   II. Series.
HT1031.F66   1983   326'.0973   83-7906
ISBN 0-8071-1118-X

TO THE MEMORY OF
W. E. B. DU BOIS

CONTENTS

ACKNOWLEDGMENTS

This book originated as the Walter Lynwood Fleming Lectures, which I delivered at Louisiana State University in March, 1982. I am deeply indebted to Professor John L. Loos and his colleagues in the history department for honoring me with the invitation to deliver the Fleming Lectures, and for the hospitality they offered while I was in Baton Rouge.

Several friends and colleagues read the manuscript and provided criticism and suggestions, from which I have benefited enormously: Robin Blackburn, LaWanda Cox, Stanley Engerman, Steven Hahn, Bruce Levine, Lawrence Powell, James P. Shenton, Fred Siegel, Judith Stein, and Michael Weisser. My parents, Jack and Liza Foner, also read the manuscript and offered sagacious advice.

I owe a special debt of gratitude to Ira Berlin and his colleagues on the Freedmen and Southern Society Project, Barbara Fields, Leslie Rowland, and Joseph Reidy, for generously sharing with me the fruits of their own path-breaking project, a documentary history of American emancipation, and for subjecting my ideas and writings to friendly criticism.

Frederick Cooper and Sidney Mintz shared with me their understanding of problems of emancipation, labor relations, and peasant societies, and made valuable criticisms of the manuscript. How strongly their writings on these subjects have influenced my own thinking should be evident in the first chapter. I also want to thank Mary Rayner, then a graduate student at Duke University, who some years ago provided me with an extensive annotated list of works on African history.

In the course of research on the Reconstruction period, I have utilized libraries throughout the United States and in England, and been treated with unfailing courtesy by librarians and archivists too numerous to list here. I do, however, want to single out for special thanks Allen Stokes of the South Caroliniana Library, and Wilma Waites of the South Carolina Archives, whose assistance has been invaluable. Lillian Feder and Helga Moody, librarians, respectively, at the City University Graduate Center and City College of New York, cheerfully complied with what must have seemed innumerable interlibrary loan requests, and I am very grateful for their assistance.

I am also indebted to Les Phillabaum and Beverly Jarrett of Louisiana State University Press for the friendly and professional way they handled the preparation of this book for publication.

Finally, my thanks to Lynn Garafola for her intellectual incisiveness, moral support, and very special comradeship.

NOTHING
BUT FREEDOM

INTRODUCTION

Among the revolutionary processes that transformed the nineteenth-century world, none was so dramatic in its human consequences or far-reaching in its social implications as the abolition of chattel slavery. Whether accomplished by black revolution, legislation, or civil war, emancipation not only eliminated an institution increasingly at odds with the moral sensibility of the age, but raised intractable questions about the system of economic organization and social relations that would replace slavery. Especially in the Western Hemisphere, plantation slavery was simultaneously a system of labor, a mode of racial domination, and the foundation upon which arose a distinctive ruling class. As a result, its demise threw open the most fundamental questions of economy, society, and polity. And in all postemancipation societies, the pivot on which social conflict turned was the new status of the former slave.

The chapters that follow explore at three levels of analysis—international, regional, and local—some of the consequences of emancipation. The first chapter examines the aftermath of slavery in Haiti and the British Caribbean, and also looks briefly at

early twentieth-century racial and economic relations in southern and eastern Africa. Despite the fact that the abolition of
forced labor has been a major theme of modern world history, it
is striking, as C. Vann Woodward observes, that "very little has
been written so far on the comparative history of emancipations
and reconstructions." This is all the more remarkable in view of
the fact that comparisons of various systems of slavery and race
relations have produced some of the most influential writings of
the past twenty years. There are, it is true, dangers in the comparative method, most notably the temptation to slight the distinctiveness of particular historical experiences in the quest for
overarching generalizations. Nonetheless, comparative analysis
permits us to move beyond "American exceptionalism" to de-
velop a more sophisticated understanding of the problem of
emancipation and its aftermath.[1]

Rather than assaying a full-scale comparative history of postemancipation societies, a task far beyond the confines of a single
essay, my purpose is to illuminate a series of interrelated historical processes and conflicts involving land, labor, and the postemancipation state that shed new light on the experience of
the United States. As in any comparative study, the choice of
subjects is, to some extent, arbitrary. My selection of Haiti
and the British Caribbean arises partly from the patterns of adjustment to emancipation witnessed in these societies, and
partly from the fact that, occurring earlier than abolition in this
country, the end of slavery there profoundly affected the ways
Americans, black and white alike, responded to their own experience of emancipation. Rather than examining subsequent
emancipations in late nineteenth-century Cuba and Brazil, I
have chosen to look instead at the process of rural class formation in southern and eastern Africa, to illustrate how the resolu-
tion of the same issues that emerged in the Caribbean—the control of labor, the distribution of land and the uses of political
power to redefine property rights, and access to economic resources—depended upon a good deal more than the moment of
abolition, or even the fact of rural laborers having once been
slaves.

After a brief description of how Caribbean emancipation affected American perceptions of slavery and abolition, the second chapter turns to how the issues and patterns prevalent in the Caribbean and Africa were duplicated in the postemancipation United States. My focus is the political economy of emancipation—how political power was employed in an attempt to redefine class relations in the aftermath of slavery. The specific issues around which political conflict revolved were often the same as those identified in Chapter One—state-sponsored immigration, laws regulating labor, taxation, the administration of justice, and the statutory definition of property rights. The American political context, however, was distinctive, for, uniquely in postemancipation societies, the former slaves during Reconstruction enjoyed universal manhood suffrage and a real measure of political power. Thus, more than in any other society experiencing the end of slavery, the state itself, for a time, became a battleground between former master and former slave.

Finally, the third chapter examines a specific set of events during American Reconstruction, the strikes of rice workers along the Combahee River in South Carolina, to illustrate how many of these same issues involving the relations between planter and laborer were resolved at the local level. Though hardly typical of the entire South, the Combahee strikes and the general fate of the postemancipation rice economy reveal how the existence of sympathetic local and state governments during Reconstruction afforded American freedmen a form of political and economic leverage unmatched by their counterparts in other societies.

The purpose of this study, then, is to examine crucial aspects of the forging of a new social order in the aftermath of slavery. I am all too aware that many essential parts of this process are, of necessity, slighted here. The evolution of a new system of race relations is not touched upon, except insofar as it involved the definition of blacks' status as free laborers. My purpose is not to pose an artificial hierarchy of importance involving race and class relations, a position untenable, at any rate, in plantation societies where race and class lines so closely overlapped and reinforced each other, but to examine the economic and political structures apart from which race relations cannot be understood. As Edgar Thompson observes, "Negroes and whites did not meet each other simply as tourists or as sightseers."[2] Their interactions were largely defined by their place in the evolving political economy. Nonetheless, the social, cultural, and ideological relations between the races certainly deserve extended study in their own right.

So too, the local experience of the rice region examined in Chapter Three needs to be supplemented by detailed examination of the adjustment to abolition in other parts of the South. The evolution of sharecropping in the cotton South has received a good deal of attention of late, but developments in the tobacco districts of the Upper South and the sugar economy of Louisiana, have only begun to be studied. In the latter case, closely supervised gang labor persisted after the end of slavery, and conflicts between planters and freedmen focused not so much on access to land, as in other parts of the South, as on the level of wages. Here a different framework of economic, technological, and ecological constraints and, perhaps, distinctive traditions among blacks and whites, produced a very different result from that outlined in my study of the rice region.[3]

The adjustment to emancipation in the American South, moreover, involved a far more complex set of class interactions than in the islands of the Caribbean. The process of emancipation unleashed forces that transformed the economy of the white upcountry, drawing that previously self-sufficient region into the cotton kingdom, and stimulating the rise of a new class of small-town merchants. Postemancipation southern politics was shaped by conflicts involving white yeomen, merchants, and an emerging industrial bourgeoisie; certainly it must be understood as more than a story of the blacks and their masters. In addition, as in every postemancipation society, outside forces affected the struggle that succeeded slavery, often decisively. The changing place of the plantation staples in the world economy, the federal presence, and the response to emancipation by various classes in the North, all contributed to the postemancipation outcome. All these issues and more must be considered if the aftermath of slavery is to be understood in its full complexity. I have touched on some of these questions in previous writings, and hope to accord them the treatment they deserve in my forthcoming general history of Reconstruction.[4] Their omission here, however, results not simply from lack of space, but from my conviction that, despite the indispensable broader context, much can be learned by isolating the struggle between former master and former slave, the focal point of conflict in the postemancipation South.

The dedication of this book is a small tribute to one of the towering figures of modern American life. Poet, activist, father of Pan-Africanism, and founder of the National Association for the Advancement of Colored People, W. E. B. Du Bois was, as well, an outstanding scholar, a pioneer in recovering and interpreting the black experience. His monumental *Black Reconstruction in America* is replete with insights, revolutionary in their implications for the scholarship of the 1930s, that have become almost commonplace today: slavery was the fundamental cause of the Civil War, blacks played a central role in that conflict and its aftermath, the land issue was crucial to the fate of Reconstruction, an account of Reconstruction based only upon the testimony of whites must be hopelessly flawed. Other insights have yet to be assimilated into the study of the period, particularly Du Bois's insistence that a full understanding of Reconstruction can only emerge from a comprehensive examination of the interests and responses of social classes north and south, laborer as well as planter and capitalist. Still other themes have helped define the agenda for the present study.

It was Du Bois, more than any other scholar, who identified the struggle over the labor of the emancipated slave as the crucial issue of Reconstruction (a point he drove home by entitling his opening chapter not "The Slave," but "The Black Worker"). And it was Du Bois who pointed to the international context of slavery and emancipation and the significance of the failure of American Reconstruction for "that dark and vast sea of human labor in China and India, the South Seas and all Africa; in the West Indies and Central America . . . that great majority of mankind."[5] Indeed, if any conviction animated Du Bois's approach, it was the essential radicalism of Reconstruction, an observa-

tion many modern scholars have unfortunately lost sight of. As
Du Bois understood and as the chapters that follow seek to demonstrate, Reconstruction, in a comparative context, stands as a
unique and dramatic experiment in interracial democracy in the
aftermath of slavery. *Black Reconstruction* has never been re-
viewed in the *American Historical Review*, the profession's pre-
mier journal.[6] Nonetheless, the book raised the questions, many
of them still unresolved, that must be answered before modern
scholars can emulate Du Bois in attempting a comprehensive
synthesis of the Reconstruction experience.

The title of this book is taken from a comment in December,
1865, by former Confederate General Robert V. Richardson,
treasurer of the American Cotton Planters' Association: "The
emancipated slaves own nothing, because nothing but freedom
has been given to them."[7] Apart from drawing attention to a
central dispute emerging from emancipation—the relationship
of the abolition (or confiscation) of property rights in slaves to
ownership of other property—the title also underscores the ambiguous nature of freedom itself. General Richardson and many
of his Radical Republican and black contemporaries, although
from very different perspectives, agreed that a definition of freedom as simply self-ownership was severely truncated, for it
threw blacks upon the free labor market impoverished, illiterate, and disadvantaged in countless other ways. Did not freedom
suggest more than simply the end of slavery, perhaps even a
right on the part of blacks to the land they had cleared and
tilled? Freedmen in the United States and elsewhere contended
that it did; General Richardson and the planter class insisted it
did not.

Yet the phrase "nothing but freedom" possesses, as well, a
certain ironic implication, for whatever its limitations, freedom
was, after all, more than nothing. Recent studies of politics,
social structure, and ideology after the Civil War have been
united by a single theme—continuity between the Old and New
South.[8] The drama of emancipation recedes into insignificance
in the face of the survival of plantation agriculture and the continuing exploitation of the black laborer. Historians impressed
with the continuities marking plantation societies before and

after the end of slavery, however, would do well to recall that to blacks, emancipation appeared as the fundamental watershed in their lives. No one put it better than Reverend E. P. Holmes, a Georgia black clergyman and former house servant, who told a congressional committee in 1883: "Most anyone ought to know that a man is better off free than as a slave, even if he did not have anything. I would rather be free and have my liberty. I fared just as well as any white child could have fared when I was a slave, and yet I would not give up my freedom."[9]

I

THE ANATOMY OF
EMANCIPATION

"Where can I find *in English* a correct history of the emancipation of the Russian serfs, and the terms of their liberation?" So wrote Radical Republican leader Thaddeus Stevens to his colleague Charles Sumner in the fall of 1865, when the terms of liberation of another emancipated people commanded the center stage of American politics. Within a few months, Stevens had located his answer. When the House of Representatives debated the Freedmen's Bureau bill in February, 1866, Stevens drew upon the Russian example to urge that provisions be added guaranteeing the freedmen ownership of land. "When that wise man the Emperor of Russia set free twenty-two million serfs," Stevens told the House, "he compelled their masters to give them homesteads upon the very soil which they had tilled . . . 'for,' said he, in noble words, 'they have earned this, they have worked upon the land for ages, and they are entitled to it.'" "The experiment," Stevens contended, "has been a perfect success."[1]

Today, historians do not share Stevens' enthusiastic appraisal of Alexander II, Czar of All the Russias, or his program of emancipation. We now know that while the freeing of the serfs dealt the Russian landed gentry a blow from which many of its members never recovered, it did not create a prosperous, independent peasantry. Emancipation left the Russian serfs "grievously disappointed"; most received plots of land too small for self-sufficient farming and, burdened with onerous redemption payments, many were forced to seek employment on the lands of their former owners.[2]

My purpose, however, is not to criticize Thaddeus Stevens for practicing history without a license, but to suggest that historians may learn something from his interest in the Russian experience. Stevens' international vision was not unique in 1865; contemporaries both black and white sensed that the experience of other societies that had undergone the social revolution known as emancipation could shed light upon the complex situation Americans confronted in the aftermath of their own Civil War. But until recently, few American historians have followed their example. "The South," Edgar Thompson observed some forty years ago, "has not been alone in its plantation experience, but most of its students and writers appear to have written and spoken as if it had," a reproach no longer applicable to the study of slavery itself, but still relevant to its aftermath.

A comparative analysis of emancipation and its legacy might well begin with Thompson's insight that the slave plantation generated, in countless local variations, a distinct system of social relations, as well as its own characteristic class system and political economy. The slave plantation served simultaneously as an agent of European colonization, a means of staple agricultural production within an expanding world capitalist market, and the incubator of a highly stratified system of race relations and a unique Afro-American culture. Because of the peculiarly authoritarian character of plantation slavery, the interdependence of its modes of political, economic, and cultural domination, emancipation unleashed conflicts that threatened to bring about changes even more far-reaching than the end of slavery itself. Central to these conflicts was the problem

Thompson identified as the outstanding single characteristic of plantation societies: their compulsive need for a disciplined, dependent labor force.[3]

Every plantation society undergoing emancipation experienced a bitter conflict over labor control or, as it might better be described, class formation—that is, the definition of the rights, privileges, and social role of a new class, the freedmen. In most cases, some form of coercion was employed in an attempt to force former slaves back to work on plantations, although no single generalization can encompass the complex patterns of labor relations that emerged in individual societies. Everywhere, the outcome of the emancipation process and the degree of autonomy achieved by the former slaves depended upon an elaborate series of power relations. Externally, the relationship of the former slave society to the larger world economy and to outside, usually colonial, political authorities, played a major role. Internally, the relative scarcity of land and labor and the degree to which, despite abolition, the planter class retained political authority, shaped the transition from slavery to freedom.

Crucial to the outcome was the nature of the abolition process itself—who controlled it, what role was played by the slaves themselves, and whether emancipation challenged the planters' hold on economic resources other than slave property, and their social and political hegemony. How effectively the power of the state was mobilized in the interest of the planter class after abolition often determined the nature of the adjustment to emancipation. Plantation slavery had always been both a political and an economic institution. It could not have existed without a host of legal and coercive measures designed to define the status of the black laborer and prevent the emergence of competing modes of social organization. As a result, the class struggle resulting from emancipation was, inevitably, politicized.

The first emancipation in the Western Hemisphere was also the most far-reaching in terms of the changed fortunes of masters and slaves. The overthrow of slavery in Saint-Domingue, the jewel of the Antilles, resulted from a black revolution in which most of the white population was massacred or fled into exile, the armies of England and France were defeated by the former slaves, and much of the countryside was laid waste. The Haitian revolution created the second independent nation in the New World and sent shock waves throughout the slave societies of the hemisphere.

Thanks to C. L. R. James and other writers, the personal and political odyssey of Toussaint L'Ouverture is now familiar. Less well known are the postemancipation social policies adopted by Toussaint and his successors. Toussaint, as James makes clear, was a man of the French Enlightenment, who envisioned independent Haiti as a multiracial society closely tied to revolutionary France. Understanding that Haiti could not stand alone in a hostile world, he sought the cooperation of the French planters. Like so many later abolitionists, moreover, Toussaint viewed the plantation as the key to the island's prosperity, and hoped to demonstrate that free men could produce the staple crops of the New World more efficiently than slaves. Fearing the freedmen would not labor voluntarily on the estates where they had been held in bondage, Toussaint in 1800 imposed a rigid system of forced labor, annulling previous sales of land to field laborers and subjecting plantation workers to military discipline. Under Jean-Jacques Dessalines, who ruled Haiti from 1804 to 1806, Toussaint's conciliatory policy toward the planters was abandoned. After the massacre of the remaining whites, the plantations fell into the hands of the state. But a Draconian labor code remained in force, since Dessalines believed only export agriculture could provide the earnings necessary to maintain a large standing army and, with it, Haitian independence.

This policy of forced labor not all that different from slavery (the lash was still employed as punishment and no provisions were made for education or political participation by the freedmen), succeeded in reviving sugar and coffee production in Haiti. But the cost was high: the complete alienation of the black masses, increasing numbers of whom abandoned the plantations to become squatters in the Haitian hills. After the assassination of Dessalines, Haiti was divided into two states, ruled by Henri Christophe and Alexander Pétion. Christophe, who declared himself emperor in 1811, continued the policy of forced labor, while Pétion took steps to attract support from the emerging peasantry by abolishing compulsory labor on the plantations and by selling land on abandoned estates. The result was the emergence of a subsistence-oriented peasantry in southern Haiti and a precipitous decline in sugar production. When Haiti was reunited, under the rule of Jean-Pierre Boyer, the "obligation to work" was again enshrined in law, with hours, wages, and strict penalties for vagrancy prescribed by the state. But Boyer's *Code Rural* was unsuccessful in reversing the emergence of the peasantry, serving only to reinforce its hostility toward the mulatto-military elite that now ruled the island.

By the 1830s, Haitian sugar production had virtually ended, although cotton and coffee were still being grown for export. Not a single plantation remained intact. Throughout the nineteenth century, Haiti had the lowest percentage of landless laborers of any Caribbean island. The Haitian freedmen had won their battle for the soil, but the outcome was, at best, a Pyrrhic victory. The history of Haiti for the remainder of the century was a melancholy saga of political instability and economic stagnation. The peasantry remained illiterate, impoverished, and politically powerless. Its lands were divided and subdivided, its economy, despite a flourishing system of internal markets, remained largely subsistence-oriented. The state's fiscal and credit policies stifled the growth of the peasant economy and turned its self-sufficiency to the advantage of a bureaucracy that saw in the masses only a source of tax revenues.[4]

The downward economic spiral that left modern Haiti as the hemisphere's poorest nation, seemed also to demonstrate to many nineteenth-century observers that a nation of ex-slave peasants must inevitably suffer economic disaster. But the lesson of Haiti was actually more ambiguous. Born in revolution, the black republic was a standing threat to the slave societies of the New World and the empires of the Old. As a result, Haiti was treated as a pariah by the international community. Recognition by France in 1824 came at the cost of an agreement to indemnify French planters for their losses, a financial burden the new nation could ill afford.[5] Like modern Cuba after its revolution, Haiti was subjected to an economic and diplomatic quarantine by former trading partners, contributing in no small measure to economic failures used, in turn, to justify the policy of international ill will.

There is an ironic footnote to the unhappy history of postemancipation Haiti, which underscores the resiliency and landhunger of the Haitian peasantry. From 1915 to 1934, more than a century after it achieved independence, Haiti was ruled by an American occupying army. Imbued with "modern" ideas about the superiority of export agriculture to peasant self-sufficiency, and convinced by the failure of Reconstruction that blacks were inherently unfit for self-government and naturally averse to productive labor, the occupation government sought to uplift the people of Haiti by reanimating the plantation system. The Haitian constitution was altered to permit alien landownership (which had been barred after the revolution), the tax structure was revised to encourage sugar production, and plans were laid to promote large-scale investment of American capital. The occupiers found the crazy-quilt pattern of landownership, whereby most peasants held their plots by custom rather than legal title, maddeningly inefficient, and moved to rationalize and modernize land titles as a prelude to inducing peasants to cede some of their holdings to foreign corporations. But lack of cooperation from the peasantry doomed the enterprise. "Barely subsisting, inarticulate, with no civil consciousness or national feeling," was how the occupation's chief financial advisor Arthur Millspaugh described them, but the Haitian peasants understood that self-sufficient agriculture, no matter how impoverished, was preferable to peonage on foreign-owned sugar estates.[6]

If the Haitian experience proved anything, it was that once destroyed (especially by its own slaves), a planter class is extremely difficult to resurrect. Attempts to use political power to restore plantation agriculture failed, despite labor policies as repressive as in any postemancipation society. In the absence of a powerful planter class, a standoff developed between state and peasant. The peasantry, lacking political power, could not use the state to bolster its own economy; the government was able to prey on the peasantry, but not destroy it. The lessons learned from the consequences of allowing former slaves access to the land were not lost on the architects of the next large-scale emancipation in the Western Hemisphere, abolition in the British Caribbean.

If in Haiti, abolition was accomplished through revolution, in the British Caribbean the process reflected all that is quintessentially English: respect for order, legal processes, and the rights of property. British emancipation not only left the planter class with its landholdings and political power intact, but provided it with twenty million pounds in compensation, so as to avoid the precedent of simply confiscating private property. Through a regressive tax system, the British working classes paid the bill for abolition. No one proposed compensating the slaves for their years of unrequited toil.[7]

The "Great Experiment" involved the emancipation of perhaps 700,000 persons, including slaves in such far-flung possessions as British Honduras, Mauritius, and the Cape of Good Hope. But the largest number were in the sugar islands, primarily Jamaica (with 311,000 slaves) and Barbados (with 83,000). Contemporaries and historians alike often described the postemancipation outcome in the sugar colonies according to a fairly simple relationship between land and labor. In small islands with high population density and little free land (Barbados, Antigua, and St. Kitts, for example), the long-established plantation system not only survived emancipation, but sugar production actually increased, since the freedmen had no alternative but to continue to labor on the estates. In British Guiana and Trinidad, with large areas of unsettled land and expanding sugar industries on the eve of abolition, blacks abandoned the plantations in large numbers, but sugar production eventually revived, employing indentured immigrants as plantation laborers. Finally, in Jamaica, with available land and an agriculture already declining before emancipation, the rise of a peasantry went hand in hand with a prolonged decline in sugar output.[8]

In various ways, therefore, most of the old British sugar areas managed to survive as plantation economies, even as expanding world demand stimulated the emergence of new areas of production. But without denying the importance of the land/labor ratio, the survival of the plantation, requiring either the denial of economic alternatives to the freedmen or an artificial increase in the supply of labor, ultimately rested on political power. Colonial and metropolitan governments alike were convinced that blacks would not work for wages on plantations without some form of coercion, and the West Indian planters, spared the bloody fate of their counterparts in Saint-Domingue, were determined to use their political hegemony to ensure the survival of the plantation economy.

The local power of the planter class, however, existed within a colonial system in which ultimate authority rested in London. On one crucial matter, British authorities and Caribbean planters agreed: the postemancipation sugar colonies should continue to be organized around the production of staple crops for export rather than self-sufficient peasant farming. But, as to how this should be accomplished, significant differences of emphasis divided London and the Caribbean.

Planters, assuming blacks were either inherently indolent or simply determined to escape plantation labor, insisted that only coercion of some kind could maintain sugar production after abolition. But British authorities, while sharing the ultimate goal of export-oriented agriculture, were reluctant to tolerate policies which would appear as a return to bondage to a public strongly influenced by the antislavery crusade. Moreover, a subtle change had taken place in British society's conception of labor itself. Almost all British economic writers had traditionally agreed that "owing to the incorrigible idleness of most labourers," wages must be kept low. Rising income would call forth not more labor, but less, a situation economists term a "backward sloping supply curve for labor," or, more simply, a "high leisure preference." As the eighteenth-century agricultural reformer Arthur Young put it, "everybody but an idiot knows that the lower classes must be kept poor or they will never be industrious." By the end of the eighteenth century, however, this view of labor had been supplanted by an alternative ideology: free market economics. For Adam Smith and his disciples, the "wants" of the poor, their desire for self-improvement, like those of other persons, were elastic, not fixed. Rather than being incorrigibly lazy, the poor would labor productively, indeed more efficiently than slaves, if offered the proper incentives.[9]

By the nineteenth century, it had become a commonplace

that high wages and free choice of employment among the working classes were the glory of the British economic system. But could such assumptions be applied to the West Indies? Planters, and many of their allies in Britain, thought not. In the debates over the adjustment to abolition, an older insistence upon the intractable laziness of the poor reasserted itself, sometimes in the guise of a theory of race and climate. Not only were blacks less "rational" economically than whites, this argument went, but the very abundance of tropical areas was a poisoned gift. Because subsistence was so easily obtainable, the ultimate stimulus to labor—fear of starvation—had little meaning in the tropics. Thus, only coercion of some kind could call forth the steady, manageable labor export agriculture required. Whether it was race, climate, or a combination of the two which supposedly rendered natives of tropical areas so "lazy," this kind of thinking would continue to be employed throughout the nineteenth and twentieth centuries to justify systems of forced labor in Africa and Asia, and it helped shape white responses to emancipation in both Britain and the West Indies.[10]

Caught between an antislavery public, a beleaguered planter class, a commitment to the idea of "free" or voluntary labor, and their own fears about the reliability of black labor after emancipation, British authorities devised a program to ease the transition from slave to free labor: apprenticeship. According to the law of 1833, all agricultural slaves were to serve a six-year apprenticeship, during which they would be paid for their labor, but they would be subject to strict regulations laid down by the colonial legislatures. The hope was that blacks would continue to work on the plantations, but would gain legal equality while at the same time developing the economic wants, the familiarity with the marketplace, which would ensure their continued, voluntary labor once emancipation was complete. The aim of the apprenticeship plan was to foster good will between planter and freedman and to remake the culture of the former slaves. Not surprisingly, the program proved a catastrophic failure.[11]

As Howard Temperly suggests, "There was something more than a little ironical in the fact that those very bodies [the colonial assemblies] which had proved most resistant to change in the past should now have so powerful a voice in determining how it was to be carried out."[12] Yet, like the victorious North in 1865, the British government was unwilling to sponsor a revolutionary transformation in the structure of government in the colonies to accompany emancipation, or to assume direct control of local legislation itself. Like their later American counterparts, the British left the administration of local affairs to the individual assemblies, within the context of general principles set down in London. Britain also appointed a number of special or "stipendiary" magistrates, analogous to Freedmen's Bureau agents in the postbellum South, to supercede local judicial authorities closely allied with the planters, and to arbitrate differences between former master and former slave.

The presence of the special magistrates was much resented by the planters, who accused them of spreading abolitionist doctrines and interfering with proper discipline on the plantations. But in reality there were too few magistrates (at their peak they numbered just 132 for the entire British Caribbean) to affect the apprenticeship system markedly.[13] Legal protection for the apprentices would have to come from London, a power the Colonial Office, at first, was not averse to exercising. In the aftermath of abolition, the planter-dominated legislatures enacted a series of laws regulating labor not unlike the South's later Black Codes. St. Kitts in 1835 made insubordination or "spreading any false report" punishable by sixty lashes and six months in prison. In Dominica, the definitions of vagrancy included making "any noise whatever in the street." Barbados made loitering on a plantation punishable by a month in prison; Jamaica designated strict legal penalties for missing work or neglecting to perform labor properly. "Insubordination" in Jamaica—an offense undefined in the statute—was punishable by thirty-nine lashes or two weeks on a penal gang. Antigua, the only sugar island choosing to move directly to full abolition without an apprenticeship period, made all contracts for labor enforceable in the courts. Most of these laws, however, were disallowed in London—they smacked too much of a return to slavery—although strict vagrancy laws were allowed to remain on the statute books.[14]

The ultimate failure of apprenticeship was inevitable, given the former slaves' aspiration to complete and immediate freedom and the planters' intention, as the governor of Barbados observed, to "cling to arbitrary power over the Negroes." The apprenticeship system sparked riots among blacks in Montserrat and St. Kitts; mounting complaints followed of insubordination, laziness, and demands for higher wages throughout the Caribbean. There were also accounts of brutal whippings and the defrauding of the apprentices by their former masters. By 1835 reports that apprenticeship was little more than another system of unrequited labor were circulating in Britain, and pressure to end the experiment was mounting. Three years later, seeing the handwriting on the wall, the colonial legislatures ended apprenticeship and decreed the complete freedom of the blacks.[15]

In large sections of the British Caribbean, the end of apprenticeship was followed by a "flight from the estates" and the rise, as in Haiti, of a black peasantry. To a certain extent, the exodus reflected a simple reality: freedom for many blacks meant dissociating themselves from the plantations. But in most cases, the rise of the peasantry resulted from a more complex series of interactions and motivations. This new peasant class emerged from bitter conflict between planter and freedman over customary property rights, and incompatible definitions of the meaning of freedom. The rise of the peasantry was as much a response to the conditions of emancipation as a legacy of slavery.[16]

The origins of the peasant class did, however, lie deep in the history of West Indian slavery. In order to reduce their own costs, planters had allowed slaves access to "provision grounds" to raise their own food. As Sidney Mintz has shown, the curious alchemy of plantation slavery transformed a burden—extra work after plantation labor was completed—into a customary right deeply valued by the slaves. In their gardens and provision plots, slaves could work independently of white supervision and in groups of their own choosing, and could sell surplus crops at local markets. The provision grounds, Mintz argues, created under slavery a "proto-peasantry" with training in the management of a small farm and in marketing practices, easing the transition to peasant farming after emancipation. They also provided a standard by which blacks defined their freedom. Whatever else it meant, freedom, they insisted, must not leave them with fewer rights, or a lower standard of living, than they had enjoyed as slaves.[17]

This, however, was precisely what many planters sought to accomplish in the aftermath of apprenticeship. Ignoring the obvious fact that the provision grounds created for many black families a strong tie to the estates, planters now sought to make the most of their new status as employers of free labor in a capitalist marketplace. Customary property rights had no place in this new order; if blacks wanted access to the provision grounds, they must pay for the privilege. Planters thus demanded exorbitant rents for the use of land and the right to live in homes often built by the blacks themselves. In many cases, the low wage rates established under apprenticeship were actually reduced. The withdrawal of customary rights was a source of conflict throughout the Caribbean. "During our slavery," a group of striking British Guiana plantation workers declared in 1842, "we was clothed, ration and seported in all manner of respects. Now we are free men (free indeed), we are to work for nothing."

Planters also resisted another nearly universal response of West Indian blacks to freedom—their attempt to reconstruct family life by withdrawing women and children from plantation field labor. On many plantations, blacks who refused to sign contracts satisfactory to the owners were summarily evicted. If the aim was to intimidate the freedmen into remaining as a docile labor force, the planters' failure was complete—in areas, that is, where land was available. In tiny Barbados the plantations continued to operate as before, but, especially in Jamaica, Trinidad, and British Guiana, there was a wholesale desertion from the estates. What one historian calls the "short-sighted and illogical actions of the planters" transformed into reality their own dire predictions about the impact of emancipation.[18]

It was Jamaica, with half the slaves in the British Caribbean, in which the rise of the peasantry had the most destructive impact upon the plantation economy. By 1861 there were some fifty thousand freeholders on the island, while fewer than half that number remained on the sugar estates. The number of plantations had fallen by half since abolition and sugar production had plummeted; only in the twentieth century would it again reach the levels of the slavery era. Meanwhile, the production of ground provisions—the yams, sweet potatoes, and arrowroot grown by the peasants—comprised an ever-increasing portion of the island's output. To many observers convinced that prosperity depended upon export agriculture, the failure of emancipation in Jamaica appeared complete.[19]

But, while its great population (and, one suspects, the "disastrous" outcome of emancipation there) encouraged British observers to equate it with the entire Caribbean, Jamaica was only part of the story. On Barbados, as we have seen, the plantations continued more or less intact, although a small group of black landowners did come into existence. In Antigua as well, there was no real change in land tenure patterns after abolition. But even here there were continuing complaints about the irregularity and unpredictability of the labor force. In the Windward and Leeward islands, planters were forced to tolerate the peasant villages that did emerge, out of fear that their labor force would emigrate to larger islands. On Trinidad peasant villages arose easily, since only one quarter of private land on the island was under cultivation and large tracts of Crown land remained open to squatters. And in British Guiana, with vast areas of unsettled land, numerous free villages arose. Here, within a decade of freedom, the village population was more than double the number remaining on the sugar estates, and, as in Jamaica, sugar production declined precipitously.[20]

The conflict between the freedmen's desire for autonomy and the planters' demand for a disciplined labor force unites the history of Caribbean societies in the aftermath of emancipation. Everywhere, planters feared the peasant villages as a challenge to their control over labor and the cause of a relentless upward pressure on the wages of those who remained. But in only a few cases were they able entirely to prevent their appearance.

The emergence and expansion of the black peasantry was the most striking change in the Caribbean social order in the aftermath of emancipation. Although oriented toward self-sufficiency, the peasants were not simply subsistence farmers. While some peasant villages sprang up on unoccupied Crown land far from roads and markets, many developed on or near the old plantations. Their material wants did expand, they saved money to build churches and educate their children, and an increasing proportion of their labor was devoted to marketable commodities like coffee, bananas, and arrowroot. In Trinidad, sugar production by the peasantry eventually eclipsed that of the estates. Most peasant holdings were acquired not by squatting, but by purchase, with funds laboriously accumulated by wage labor or marketing, often through informal cooperative associations, friendly societies, and church groups. Blacks may not have been "rational economic men" in the sense understood by classical economics (that is, willing, disciplined wage laborers), but this reflected not an aversion to labor, but the desire to labor under circumstances of their own choosing.[21]

Like peasants everywhere, those of the Caribbean, despite a measure of autonomy inconceivable under slavery, often found themselves at the mercy of the elements, the world market, and hostile political authorities, foreclosing the possibility of substantial economic advance. Large numbers continued to work irregularly or seasonally on the sugar estates. In times of drought, peasants avidly sought plantation employment; in good times, the planters complained of a scarcity of wage labor. In Jamaica particularly, whose planters found it difficult to compete with heavily capitalized sugar production in Cuba and Brazil, there was a constant downward pressure on plantation wages throughout the postemancipation decades.[22]

To a considerable extent, the fate of the Caribbean peasantries rested on both their access to the scarce resources of these economies, and their ability to maintain the labor shortage that followed closely upon emancipation throughout the Caribbean. By the same token, planters recognized in the labor question the key to the maintenance of their own social order. In the densely populated smaller islands, the labor problem was "solved" by the unavailability of land for the freedmen. In Trinidad and British Guiana, planters turned to the importation of large numbers of indentured laborers to redress the imbalance in the labor market and preserve the plantation system.

"For nearly one hundred years," Walter Rodney has written

of British Guiana, "sugar planters bitterly resisted the creation of a free labor market as implied by Emancipation." Indentured labor was one means of resistance. The relative balance of freedom and coercion in indentured labor contracts has long been a matter of dispute. Some contract laborers were truly voluntary, while others were little more than kidnapping victims. But, clearly, what made indentured laborers attractive was that they were less free than the former slaves. Indeed, it was this obvious fact that led the British government to react warily when Caribbean planters first sought to import plantation laborers. In the early 1840s, British authorities restricted contracts to a term of one year, but official opinion gradually embraced the planters' view that immigration under long-term indenture was essential to resolve the West Indian labor crisis. Eventually, the "coolies," most of them from India, were obligated to work for five years, with another five-year term required for free passage home. Their subordinate status was defined by local law: criminal penalties for breach of the indenture, fines for absence from work, and legally stipulated work quotas.[23]

By the 1850s, large-scale importation of Indian immigrants had begun, and it did not end until World War I. Between 1838 and 1865, nearly 100,000 Indians were introduced into the British Caribbean; all told, British Guiana imported 200,000 and Trinidad 150,000. The trade did not, in fact, reach its peak until the 1880s and 1890s, long after it had succeeded in stabilizing the plantation economy, for planters valued it as a means of depressing the wage level for the entire society. As one British Guiana planter explained, "So long as an estate has a large Coolie gang, Creoles must give way in prices asked."[24]

If slavery was the characteristic labor system of the first Age of Empire, indentured labor was inconceivable apart from a new era of imperialism. The trade in "coolies," the nineteenth century's replacement for the trans-Atlantic slave trade, could not have existed without the expansion and consolidation of the overseas empires of Britain and other European nations. Over one million Indians and a quarter of a million Chinese, plus lesser numbers of Japanese and Pacific islanders, became its victims, and old plantation systems like those of Mauritius, Trinidad, and British Guiana, and new ones including Ceylon, Malaya, Fiji, and Hawaii, came to depend on the trade for a labor supply. The British government allowed other nations to acquire contract laborers in India, so that, in the Western Hemisphere, Dutch Surinam and the French sugar islands also imported their quota. Peruvian sugar planters and guano producers brought in nearly 100,000 Chinese between 1850 and 1874, and 125,000 were introduced into Cuba. Although there was a growing chorus of protest against the "coolie" trade in England, it was finally swept away because of an upsurge of hostile opinion not in Britain, but in colonial India. It never aroused quite the hostility of the slave trade, partly because the contract laborers were in fact paid wages, and partly because the spread of imperialism went hand in hand with broad acceptance of racist ideas concerning tropical peoples and their reluctance to labor.[25]

The use of government-sponsored indentured immigration to transform the labor market and labor relations is a striking example of how the power of the state helped to determine the ultimate fate of planters and freedmen in the postemancipation Caribbean. The land/labor ratio, as we have seen, was crucial in determining postabolition class relations, but so too was the political context. Emancipation in the British Caribbean did not challenge the local political hegemony of the planter class. The right to vote in the West Indies remained severely restricted, although in view of the narrow basis of the franchise in England, British authorities did not consider it unfair. Free mulattoes had been accorded equal political rights on the eve of abolition throughout the Caribbean, but property qualifications effectively excluded the mass of the freedmen from the suffrage. In British Guiana, according to one observer, government was "neither Crown Colony Government nor Representative Government, but a travesty of both." At the end of the nineteenth century, when the colony's population stood at 270,000, the electorate numbered 2,046. The same situation existed elsewhere. In the 1850s, of a Barbadian population of 150,000, only 147 voted in one election. Grenada, with 32,600 inhabitants, had 191 electors; St. Vincent, with the same population, had 273.[26]

In the largest island, Jamaica, planters persistently sought to increase property qualifications in order to exclude the peasantry from voting. With a population which reached 500,000 in the 1860s, the number of voters never exceeded 3,000. The property qualification was not the only means of restricting the franchise, indeed many black peasants held enough land to qualify. Apathy certainly played a part in the peasants' exclusion from political life, but so did the various poll taxes and legal regulations which, as one observer noted, "almost require a man to keep a lawyer to look after his vote."[27]

Throughout the Caribbean, then, planters enjoyed a virtually free hand, so long as the rarely invoked British veto was avoided, in employing political authority to bolster their beleaguered economic position. The variety of means they adopted to create a labor force and to restrict the growth of the peasant villages, demonstrated the resourcefulness and vindictiveness of a class that believed its very survival to be at stake. The legal code, taxation policies, government expenditures, and the administration of justice were all molded with one idea in mind: to maintain the plantation economy.

The one type of legislation which, at least at the outset, provoked British intervention, was that directly controlling the black labor force. In the aftermath of apprenticeship, planter-dominated assemblies enacted a series of laws restricting the freedom of movement of the former slaves, placing vagrants on penal gangs, and imposing heavy fines for work deemed insufficient by the employer. Many such measures, brought to the attention of the Colonial Office by abolitionists, were overturned in London. Yet local judicial authority remained completely in the hands of planters. With emancipation, indeed, there was a considerable expansion of the size and cost of the judiciary. Under slavery according to one contemporary, there had been "no magistrates, and no police"; crime was dealt with by the individual planter. Now, the judiciary became a major means of disciplining the black labor force. Heavy fines for vagrancy, theft, and trespass were routinely imposed on the freedmen. Later in the century, after British vigilance had diminished, British Guiana made virtually any labor recalcitrance a criminal offense, and used the courts to police the indentured immigrants, over 65,000 of whom were convicted of breach of contract in the last quarter of the century. It would be wrong, of course, to assume that every repressive law on the statute books was effectively enforced. The police and judicial systems could lodge men in jail, but forcing them to work efficiently on the plantations, or even evicting them from unoccupied land, would have required a police force far larger and more expensive than anything existing in the British Caribbean. The law could, however, be effective in reducing the economic opportunities available to blacks, and inhibiting the growth, if not the existence, of peasant agriculture.[28]

Throughout the Caribbean, taxation was also employed to limit the freedmen's access to land, to restrict the economic progress of the peasantry, and to induce blacks to labor for wages. The burden of taxation, borne mostly by the planters during slavery, was shifted to weigh most heavily upon the freedmen. Taxes on imported food, animals and wagons, and on small holdings of land, were a constant burden to peasant agriculture, while items of importance to the planters, ranging from diamonds and books to cattle and sheep, were generally exempted from import duties. Costly licenses were required for the local marketing of sugar and coffee, and poll taxes were instituted in an attempt to force freedmen to engage in cash-oriented labor. In Jamaica and throughout the Caribbean, planters escaped with light taxation, while "the heaviest burden [fell] on the poorest class."[29]

If the incidence of taxes was grossly unfair, so too was the appropriation of the monies raised. The most striking example was the use, in Trinidad and British Guiana, of public funds to subsidize the importation of contract laborers. In effect, the freedmen, through taxation, financed the bringing in of laborers whose purpose was to reduce their own standard of living. Here, too, where lands near the sea were protected from inundation only by an elaborate system of dikes, legislative appropriations for dams and drainage went almost entirely to the plantations. The peasant villages had to bear the heavy cost of sea defense themselves.

The largest items in the postemancipation budgets of the sugar colonies were the police and judicial systems, followed by government subventions to indentured immigration. Education was accorded little attention, and, while the established Anglican church received funds, black religious organizations did not. Government capital was provided to enable sugar planters to finance a technological revolution in sugar production, but the building of roads and bridges to assist peasants in marketing their crops was neglected, and planters opposed appropriations to enterprises like railroad construction, fearing they might draw laborers away from the estates.[30]

In most of the Caribbean, as we have seen, property qualifications prevented the growth of real political opposition to planter control. Peasant indifference also appears to have played a part. In British Guiana, according to Alan Adamson, "the great mass of the villagers remained apathetic to all but the impact of immediate, parochial experience." Their main desire, it appears, was to be left alone. But in Jamaica, within a generation after emancipation, a political challenge to planter rule did emerge, which transformed the balance of political power in the British Caribbean.

Less isolated from the mainstream of their society than their British Guiana counterparts, the Jamaican peasantry had nonetheless taken little part in politics before the 1850s. The indigenous mulatto class, unlike its counterpart in American Reconstruction, made little initial effort to mobilize the freedmen for political purposes. But, beginning in the 1850s, a group of colored leaders of the Town party (a loose coalition of the free colored elite with Jewish merchants and town professionals) began to appeal actively for the votes of blacks who owned sufficient land to meet the property qualification. Although the Town party had previously ignored the needs of the peasantry, doing nothing, for example, to extend roads or credit to the villages, it now pressed for a reform of taxation and franchise requirements in the interests of the freedmen, and spoke confidently of a new Jamaica ruled by blacks and browns. The prospect of a black electoral majority terrified Jamaica's planters, who immediately increased the property qualification for voting, and was not greeted with enthusiasm in London.[31]

The climax of the political crisis of the 1860s in Jamaica was the Morant Bay "Rebellion" of 1865, when a crowd of blacks stormed a courthouse to protest the harsh sentences being meted out to squatters by local magistrates who were also prominent planters. The chief magistrate and fifteen other men were killed in the riot. In retaliation, Governor Edward John Eyre ordered a brutal suppression, including the burning of peasant villages and the execution of over four hundred blacks. A culmination of tensions produced by political conflict and an economic depression, the Morant Bay affair reinforced planter fears that a future peasant democracy might assume control of the legislature. In an ironic reversal of our own Compromise of 1877—in which "home rule" for the South cemented sectional reconciliation—the Jamaica Assembly voted itself out of existence, and the island became a Crown colony, ruled directly from London. Planters on the other islands quickly concluded that their interests, as well, would be safer in the long run under British rule than with even a semblance of democracy at home. After all, as one historian puts it, "the unenfranchised Negro in the West Indies would certainly have no chance of unseating a government in Britain." All the sugar islands except Barbados followed suit, and representative government, for the time being, expired. The result was the political demoralization of a generation of blacks and a reversion of full political control of the islands to Britain.[32]

The planters' willingness to entrust their fate to Westminster reveals how far British colonial policy itself had evolved since emancipation. As in the United States, an initial period of genuine concern for the well-being of the former slaves, tempered however by a commitment to the continuation of export-oriented agriculture, was succeeded by growing indifference or outright hostility concerning the freedmen, punctuated by occasional efforts to protect their minimal rights. The rise of the Caribbean peasantry accelerated the change in British policy, as well as the recognition of the fundamental community of interests between metropolitan and colonial capital.

The 1830s had been a period of considerable ill will between Caribbean planters and the Colonial Office, which, in the planters' view, took far too seriously its responsibility for protecting the rights of the former slaves. Some London officials, like Henry Taylor, head of the Colonial Office's West India Department, unsuccessfully advocated direct rule from London, believing local assemblies were incapable of "justice or humanity to the negroes," while the freedmen were too recently removed from slavery to be trusted with political power. It was self-defeating, Taylor believed, to "force this social change and yet to leave the political framework of this totally different society the same as it was." But his plan for the abolition of the West Indian assemblies was torpedoed during the political crisis in Britain which coincided with the end of apprenticeship. The outcome was a victory for the Jamaica planters and the removal of the threat of regular interference from London in the affairs of the islands.[33]

During the 1840s and 1850s, both the humanitarian spirit and British interest in the colonies faded. Apart from the occasional invalidation of individual pieces of legislation, the Colonial Office paid little attention to the islands, and the assemblies enjoyed a free hand in regulating their own affairs. Increasingly, moreover, British authorities came to realize that the fundamental assumption they shared with the planters—that the plantation should continue to dominate West Indian society—required some limitation on the freedom of the former slaves. The emerging peasantry was seen in London, as in the Caribbean, as a threat not simply to the economic well-being of the islands, but to civilization itself. Removed from the influence of whites, this argument went, blacks would relapse into African barbarism. Reports of widespread reluctance to labor and of the revival of African religious cults raised the specter of a second Haiti, where, supposedly, Western civilization had vanished. Neither planter nor government seriously considered promoting the economic development of the Caribbean along the lines of peasant production.

There were, on occasion, glimmers of an alternative point of view. Lord Harris, arriving as governor in Trinidad in 1846, proposed a far-reaching plan for rural development, which would have made Crown lands available to groups of peasants at nominal prices, but the planter interest was able to block its implementation. Each year, concludes William Green's recent study of British emancipation, the London authorities conceded more and more to the planters—on police, the franchise, indentured immigration, and labor legislation—while abolitionist protests were ignored. By the time of Morant Bay, even Henry Taylor was convinced emancipation had failed and that the freedmen, misled by "wild black missionaries," had descended into "debauchery," vagrancy, and plots to slaughter the whites and take possession of the plantations. Thus, the coming of Crown colony status did not signal any significant change in economic and social policy in the Caribbean, but simply a shift of political power beyond the reach of the freedmen, the better to guarantee the survival of the plantation system.[34]

What, then, were the lessons of West Indian emancipation? This question would be a major point of debate throughout the nineteenth century. In 1839, considering the prospect of abolition in the French colonies, Alexis de Tocqueville, like so many of his countrymen before and since, urged France to profit from the mistakes of the British. Tocqueville concluded from recent events that some kind of transitional period after abolition was necessary to prevent the collapse of the plantations, but he identified the reason for the failure of apprenticeship: it had been too similar to slavery in the eyes of the blacks. No less committed than his British counterparts to maintaining plantation agriculture (he even proposed an outright ban on black acquisition of land for five years), Tocqueville still recognized that, to win the confidence of the freedmen, it was necessary to "destroy every relation which has existed between the master and the slave." To accomplish this, the state must step between the two parties, becoming "the sole guardian of the enfranchised population; it should grant the services of the blacks to the planters on its own conditions." Otherwise, the blacks would revert to barbarism and idleness, a serious danger, Tocqueville believed, "because France labors to create civilized societies, not hordes of savages."[35]

This equating of labor with civilization and idleness (including peasant production) with savagery, also affected the British response to emancipation. The decline of sugar production in Jamaica proved a serious embarrassment to abolitionists. By the

1860s, the "failure" of emancipation had become one foundation for a new and virulent strain of British racism. As the rising young Liberal politician Charles Dilke observed, "If it is still impossible openly to advocate slavery in England, it has, at least, become a habit persistently to write down freedom." The Morant Bay "rebellion" confirmed the view that blacks were inherently incapable of self-government. Events, the *Daily Telegraph* declared, had proved "that the negro is still a savage." Coinciding with violence in Ireland and the Hyde Park riots in London, Morant Bay played its part in a general hardening of both class and racial attitudes and a retreat from egalitarianism among the British middle class.[36]

The ironies here are indeed striking. For, at the very time Caribbean peasants were being arraigned for relapsing into barbarism, a growing strand in English middle-class thought was exalting land reform as a means of weakening the power of the British landed aristocracy and creating a new class of yeoman farmers. The "rehabilitation of the peasant proprietor," associated most fully with John Stuart Mill, held up the family farmers of Switzerland, Holland, and France as models of economic efficiency and public virtue, illustrations of "the magic of property." But such assumptions did not extend to the blacks of the Caribbean; their desire to escape plantation labor and acquire land was perceived as incorrigible idleness.[37]

Just as Americans began their own confrontation with the consequences of emancipation, respectable British opinion concluded that blacks were incapable of self-government. As the *Contemporary Review* put it, "only the preponderance of an Anglo-Saxon element guarantees an inherent capacity for freedom." As America embarked upon an unprecedented experiment in interracial democracy in Reconstruction, Britain installed "semi-despotic government" in her Caribbean colonies. To the British, the West Indian experience demonstrated the need for "strong government" over "uncivilized peoples." A generation later, as Britain expanded her dominion over African societies, the lessons of the West Indies would not be forgotten.[38]

A brief look, indeed, at British southern and eastern Africa around the turn of this century, reveals a complex process of class formation and a set of relationships involving land, labor, and the state, instructive in both their similarities and differences with the Caribbean experience. With the exception of Zanzibar, where slavery was abolished in 1897, and coastal Kenya, where it survived until 1907, the "labor problem" in southern and eastern Africa involved not the consequences of the emancipation of the slave, but the emancipation of the land from black ownership, not inhibiting a propertyless group of freedmen from obtaining land, but dispossessing a peasantry with a preexisting stake in the soil. But the aim of British imperial policy and local elites was essentially the same as in the Caribbean—that is, the making of a reliable, dependent wage labor force. Remarkably similar policies toward that end were adopted in South Africa, Rhodesia, and Kenya. The final results revealed both the power and the limitations of state action, and the conditions under which most African peasants were, in the end, proletarianized.[39]

Ironically, the peasantry whose destruction was deemed indispensable to the establishment of a black working class for white-owned mines and farms, had itself been called into existence by the earlier expansion of colonial settlement. Recent research has detailed the process by which capitalism first created and then destroyed the peasantry of southern and eastern Africa. The spread of diamond and gold mining and white farming in the late nineteenth and early twentieth centuries created a market for foodstuffs to which African farmers often responded more effectively than white settlers. African society was already deeply involved in local exchange relations; the growth of the white population simply expanded the market for milk, grain, and cattle. The peasants, many of whom were in fact living on white-owned land for which they owed rent or labor service, also provided a growing market for manufactured goods supplied by European merchants. But this increasingly affluent peasantry resisted efforts to attract it into the wage labor force.

While merchants, who found a profitable market among the peasants, and absentee landlords, who preferred to rent rather than cultivate their holdings, saw no threat in the growth of the peasantry, mine owners and cultivating farmers insisted upon the need to compel the Africans to work for wages. The process was carried out most completely in South Africa where, whatever their differences on other matters, both Afrikaaners and British settlers supported the creation of a dependent African labor force. Afrikaaner farmers had long feared the African peasantry; the discovery of gold in 1886, "the central event in the development of South Africa," as Freda Troup puts it, led to the emergence of a powerful capitalist class, closely linked with local political authorities, whose enterprises had an almost insatiable demand for cheap labor. With Africans economically successful but politically impotent, aggrieved whites—forging a distinctive alliance of "gold and maize"—turned to the state to break the back of the African peasantry.[40]

British solicitude for the fate of dark-skinned laborers having long since faded, settler complaints of the intractable laziness of African peasants met a sympathetic response in London. The experience of Caribbean emancipation and, occasionally, American Reconstruction, was cited to demonstrate that if Africans would not volunteer their labor in the marketplace, they must be coerced into doing so. As in the West Indies, British and local authorities in southern and eastern Africa called forth an array of weapons—taxation, education, and labor laws—to compel Africans to enter the labor market. The burden of taxation, as in the Caribbean, was shifted from the land and capital of white farmers and mine owners onto the African population. Hut taxes, poll taxes, and taxes on African cattle, by creating a need for cash income, sought to induce Africans to present themselves for wage labor. "We consider," said the governor of Kenya in 1913, "that taxation is the only possible method of compelling the native to leave his reserve for the purpose of seeking work. . . . Only in this way can the cost of living be increased for the native."[41]

Taxation has always been the state's weapon of last resort in the effort to promote market relations within peasant societies. By itself, however, it is not always an efficient means of bringing a wage labor force into being. Peasants could expand their production of cash crops to meet the tax burden, remaining independent of the labor market. Increasing involvement with the marketplace did, however, make many peasants increasingly vulnerable to the marketing and credit monopolies enjoyed by whites, and at the same time fostered an increase in class stratification within African communities, with poorer peasants finding themselves compelled to rely at least partially upon wage labor to survive.[42]

In the end, however, only the direct expropriation of African land "solved" the labor problem. The most famous such measure, the South African Land Act of 1913, a culmination and codification of previous efforts to undermine the peasant sector, defined the great bulk of that nation as an area where Africans were forbidden to acquire property. It became the model for subsequent legislation in Kenya and Northern and Southern Rhodesia as well, outlawing the renting or selling of land to blacks and many sharecropping and labor-tenancy arrangements. Such acts were intended to uproot large numbers of Africans from their farms and, coupled with criminal penalties for breach of contract, apprenticeship systems for black children, and pass regulations, to proletarianize the African peasantry. The South African Land Act became the foundation of the comprehensive system of racial oppression known as apartheid, but its origins lay not simply in the realm of racial ideology, significant as that was, but in the labor demands of white farmers and the diamond and gold mines. The aim was not so much to separate the races as to ensure that their continuing contact took place on terms dictated by certain classes of whites, not by Africans, not even by the impersonal marketplace.[43]

In southern and eastern Africa, the attack on the African peasantry ushered in a new phase of the prolonged struggle over land and labor, racial and class relations. Dispossession was most complete in South Africa, where a large white population widely diffused throughout the countryside, a powerful capitalist class in the mining industry and, after 1910, a modern, independent state, combined to exert a power Africans found nearly impossible to resist, although in some parts of the country peasant production remained viable into the 1930s. In Southern Rhodesia, a rapidly expanding class of white tobacco farmers and cattle grazers, closely allied with colonial authorities, succeeded by the end of the 1930s in shattering "all vestiges of African economic independence." In Northern Rhodesia and coastal Kenya, however, the land and labor laws had a far more limited impact. Here the white settler population remained small, many land speculators and landlords continued to derive income from renting land to Africans, despite the protests of white farmers, and British authorities, obsessed with keeping the cost of colonial administration as low as possible, considered laws requiring an extensive police network unfeasible. Facing perennial budget deficits, the government lacked the resources to launch massive programs of labor recruitment and repression and Africans were able to resist complete separation from their land. Nor did British authorities attempt to replicate the Belgians in the Congo, the Portuguese in Angola, or the descendants of American black émigrés in Liberia, all of whom imposed outright forced labor on Africans. Perhaps antislavery ideology played too prominent a part in justifying British penetration of Africa to make such programs acceptable.[44]

Apart from being a particularly brutal example of the use of political power to redefine economic relationships, the rise and fall of the African peasantry, like the experience of freedmen in the Caribbean, raises questions about that focal point of nineteenth-century political debate, land reform. To black and white, abolitionist, freedman and planter, access to the land appeared as the crucial issue unresolved by emancipation. As the Brazilian abolitionist Joaquim Nabuco observed, "Freeing the Negro without freeing the land is but half an abolition."[45]

But as the Caribbean and African experiences make clear, and as twentieth-century literature on land reform underscores, ownership of land was not necessarily a panacea for the economic plight of postemancipation blacks. In Haiti, a hostile world and a predatory state made land ownership little more than an economic dead end. In British Guiana and Jamaica, the planters' dominance of state government and the economy stunted the development of the peasant villages. Studies of numerous attempts at land reform in this century, in societies ranging from Latin America to Asia and Eastern Europe, conclude that where political power, the tax system, control of credit, access to markets, supplies of seeds and fertilizer, and other "factors of production" remain in hostile hands, land reform can be a "hollow victory." To accomplish its professed goals of redistributing rural income and increasing agricultural productivity, land reform must be accompanied by massive and continuing government programs of education, credit provision, and rural development, all of which are impossible where political power rests with classes that are at worst hostile and at best indifferent to the fate of the rural population. Land, in other words, is not the only scarce resource in most rural societies, and access to other resources, particularly capital, often remains highly unequal even after a land reform program is in place.[46]

Under certain circumstances, in fact, the provision of small plots of land to the agricultural population can actually serve the interests of employers of labor. Recent studies have called attention to the "articulation" between peasant and capitalist modes of production in rural societies—that is, the ways in which these forms of social organization interact with and reinforce one another. A challenge to "dual economy" models, which see the subsistence smallholder and large-scale market-oriented farmer as essentially independent, this newer work stresses that plantations, mines, and other enterprises can benefit from their relationship with a peasant sector, so long as the economic opportunities open to the peasantry are kept within carefully defined bounds. In South Africa, the reserve system did not totally dispossess the African peasantry; by allowing it access to a limited amount of poor quality land, it forced upon the African population part of the cost of feeding itself, enabling employers to pay wages below subsistence. In the Caribbean as well, some planters found that allowing freedmen access to tiny plots of land created a nearby population forced by their limited economic resources to work for wages at least part of the year. Some of the efficiencies of peasant agriculture, in other words, can, in certain circumstances, be made to help subsidize large-scale plantation agriculture.[47]

My intention here is not to denigrate land reform, but to suggest some problems that often limit its economic impact. As Thaddeus Stevens recognized, the confiscation of plantations and their distribution among the freedmen would have profoundly affected every aspect of southern life and politics. Indeed, the noneconomic results of land reform, particularly the destruction of the land-based political power of traditional agrarian ruling classes, and a change in the self-conception of those who acquire land, are often more lasting than any marked improvement in the standard of living of the rural poor. As one Caribbean planter complained, from access to land flowed "a marked diminution of the deference which [ex-slaves] have hitherto been accustomed to pay to those in authority over them," leading the blacks to consider themselves "upon a footing of equality with their employers."[48]

Throughout the Caribbean and southern and eastern Africa, planters, farmers, and mineowners continued to fear the peasant sector, no matter how cramped its opportunities for development. Access to land gave even the poorest blacks some measure of choice as to whether, when, and under what circumstances to present themselves in the labor market. But given the overall political economy of plantation regions, such autonomy tended to be at best defensive, rather than the springboard from which a sustained transformation of the rural sector could be launched. Where political power rested in hostile hands, peasants, unlike planters and white farmers, could not use the state to attempt to compensate for their own economic weaknesses and the disadvantageous position of their society within the world economy.[49]

What conclusions, then, ought we to draw from this saga of emancipation, conflict, and rural class formation? In 1843 Tocqueville observed, "If the Negroes have the right to become free, the colonists have the incontestable right not to be ruined by the Negroes' freedom." And almost everywhere, with the notable exception of Haiti, the plantation system did, in one way or another, survive the end of slavery. The persistence of the plantation did not always mean the survival of the planter class of slavery days. In many areas after emancipation, competition from new beet sugar regions and the increasing capital requirements of modern sugar technology led to the displacement of smaller, old-fashioned planters by giant firms like Tate and Lyle and United Fruit. Those planters who endured did so only as dependents of these new firms which engrossed vast tracts of land, employed advanced manufacturing techniques, and often utilized both wage and indentured labor on their holdings. The plantation system's survival and continued dominance, however, had little to do with superior economic efficiency. Indeed, in the literature on other societies' postemancipation adjustments, one massive abstraction which has commanded so much attention and debate in the United States—the free market— is conspicuous by its absence. Dominant classes everywhere feared the market, in labor, land, and credit, and used political power to suppress, as far as possible, its operations. It was control over land, credit, and marketing, all cemented by a monopoly of political power, which enabled the plantation system to survive.[50]

The dead weight of the past, as Karl Marx wrote, "weighs like a nightmare on the brain of the living."[51] Emancipation, in nearly every society where it has occurred, seems a striking illustration of this dictum. A rigid social and political dichotomy between former master and former slave, an ideology of racism, a dependent labor force with limited economic opportunities— these and other patterns seem always to survive the end of slavery, leading some theorists to minimize the consequences of emancipation altogether, positing instead an unchanging plantation structure in which slavery appears as simply one among a number of alternative labor systems.

The historian, however, ought to be suspicious of any model that views continuity rather than change as the essence of the historical experience, while ignoring the active participation of the former slaves themselves in shaping the legacy of emancipation.[52] "The objectives of the freedmen and planters," one study of Caribbean emancipation concludes, "were incompatible," and if there is one constant which unites the various adjustments to the end of slavery it is precisely their ongoing if unequal conflict. Everywhere, emancipation was succeeded by struggle for control of the scarce resources of plantation economies, paramount among them, the labor of the former slaves themselves. Lacking political power, freedmen employed the labor shortage as their principal weapon—a weapon inconceivable apart from emancipation. Long after abolition, and despite the importation of hundreds of thousands of indentured laborers, Caribbean planters continued to complain of a labor shortage— a shorthand way of describing the ways freedmen sought to determine the conditions, rhythms, and compensation of the work of themselves and their families.

For those who wish to employ the insights derived from an analysis of emancipation in other settings to illuminate the American experience, then, certain patterns stand out in bold relief.[53] The effort to create a dependent labor force, the ideological conflict over changing definitions of labor and property, the impact of metropolitan policies, the place of the society in the larger world economy, and the uses of the state in bolstering the plantation regime, all shaped the postemancipation outcome. And so too did the ongoing struggle between freedman and planter, which continued on the plantations and in peasant villages in forms both subtle and dramatic, long after slavery itself had become just a memory.

II

THE POLITICS OF
FREEDOM

At first glance, the scale, manner, and consequences of emancipation in the United States appear historically unique. The nearly four million slaves liberated in this country far outnumbered those in the Caribbean and Latin America. Although no abolition was entirely without violence, only in Haiti and the United States did the end of slavery result from terrible wars in which armed blacks played a crucial part. The economies of the Caribbean islands, tiny outposts of empire, had little in common with the nineteenth-century United States, where slavery existed within a rapidly expanding capitalist economic order.

Politically, the cast of characters in the United States was far more complex than in the West Indies. American blacks were outnumbered, even in the South, by whites, but this white population was divided against itself. There are few parallels in other postemancipation societies to the southern whites who cooperated politically with the freedmen, or the northerners, variously numbered at between twenty and fifty thousand, who moved into the South after the Civil War, carrying with them a

39

triumphant free-labor ideology and, for a time, playing a pivotal role in political affairs. Nor were there counterparts to the Radical Republicans of the North, a group with real if ultimately limited political power, which sought to forge from emancipation a thoroughgoing political and social revolution, supplanting plantation society, as one put it, by "small farms, thrifty villages, free schools, . . . respect for honest labor, and equality of political rights."

Finally and most strikingly, the United States was the only society where the freed slaves, within a few years of emancipation, enjoyed full political rights and a real measure of political power. Limited as its accomplishments may appear in retrospect, Black Reconstruction was a stunning experiment in the nineteenth-century world, the only attempt by an outside power in league with the emancipated slaves to fashion an interracial democracy from the ashes of slavery.[1]

Despite these and other exceptional features of their national experience, nineteenth-century Americans sensed that prior emancipations held lessons for the aftermath of slavery in this country. Their precise significance, however, was a matter of some dispute. As John Dickinson had said at the Constitutional Convention of 1787, "experience must be our only guide"; but the experience of Caribbean emancipation was interpreted through the lens of rival American ideologies concerning race and slavery. For southern whites, the lesson of the West Indies was unmistakable: emancipation was a failure.[2]

The consequences of abolition in Haiti and the British Caribbean played a small but noteworthy part in antebellum discussions of slavery. The overthrow of slavery in Haiti and the massacre of the whites there sent shock waves through the South and unleashed a flood of refugees who, as William Freehling notes, "served as constant reminders that servile insurrections *could* succeed." Equally pervasive was the influence of the "Great Experiment"—British emancipation—upon the southern mind. Through articles in the southern press, the dispatches of Robert M. Harrison, the Virginia-born American consul at Kingston, Jamaica, and the writings of proslavery ideologues, the lesson of the Caribbean was hammered home: "The manumitted negro will not work." Caribbean emancipation was a symbol and a warning to the white South, a demonstration of the futility of all schemes to elevate the black and of the dire fate awaiting American planters and their world in the event of abolition. As George Fitzhugh summarized this view in 1850: "The emancipation of the slaves in the West Indies is admitted to have been a failure in all respects. The late masters have been ruined, the liberated slaves refuse to work, and are fast returning to a savage state, and England herself has sustained a severe blow in the present diminution and prospective annihilation of the once enormous imports from her West Indian colonies."[3]

To American abolitionists, on the other hand, West Indian emancipation was an inspiration rather than an embarrassment, an example of what a minority could achieve through years of agitation, and a vindication of the blacks' capacity for freedom. Particularly in the first years of the Civil War, abolitionists marshaled statistics to demonstrate that emancipation in the islands had in fact succeeded. The rise of the Jamaican peasantry, they insisted, reflected not incorrigible laziness, but the intolerable working conditions demanded by the planters and a laudable ambition to become landed proprietors. "The negroes," according to one defense of the "Great Experiment," simply acted "as Englishmen or Americans similarly situated would . . . preferring an independent to a servile position, . . . exhibiting themselves to be an industrious rather than an indolent people." Others argued that, despite the decline in sugar exports, the overall standard of living in Jamaica, as measured by the spread of education, the stability of family life, and the level of subsistence, had markedly improved in the aftermath of slavery.[4]

If the attention of white abolitionists was focused on Jamaica, many black Americans found in Haiti an unrivaled inspiration. Blacks celebrated August 1, the anniversary of British West Indian emancipation, as a kind of national holiday in the years before the Civil War, but it was Haiti that proved that the world could be turned upside down. A study of black American attitudes toward Haiti remains to be written, but it seems clear that throughout the nineteenth century, Haiti stood as an example of black heroism, resiliency, and self-reliance. Whatever its failings, the black nation of Haiti had at least managed to survive in a hostile white world. The black press featured articles on Toussaint L'Ouverture, and slave rebels like Gabriel Prosser and Denmark Vesey found in Haiti a source of inspiration. (Of Vesey, his lieutenant Gullah Jack said, "He was in the habit of reading to me all the passages in the newspapers that related to St. Domingo.") In the 1850s black emigrationists saw in Haiti a possible homeland for black Americans.[5]

With the end of slavery in the United States, the practice of drawing lessons from the Caribbean experience became even more widespread. To abolitionists, the West Indies revealed the dangers of leaving the fate of the emancipated blacks in the hands of their former owners. If British emancipation was open to criticism, it was for not going far enough. "England," the Boston cotton manufacturer and Republican reformer Edward Atkinson wrote, "after she had caused the negroes to cease to be chattels, stopped far short of making them men, leaving them subject to oppressive laws made entirely under the influence of their former owners." His Boston colleague, railroad entrepreneur John Murray Forbes, likewise warned that Americans should take heed of "Jamaica's former experience in legislating the blacks back into slavery, by poor laws, vagrant laws, etc." Another abolitionist cited the Morant Bay "rebellion" of 1865 to demonstrate Britain's "grave mistakes" in attempting to create a halfway house between slavery and complete civil and political equality for blacks. Even Toussaint now came in for censure, for what Lydia Maria Child called "his favorite project of conciliating the old planters." Toussaint's mistake, Child believed, lay in "a hurry to reconstruct, to restore outward prosperity," rather than attempting radically to transform his society on the basis of free labor principles. The implications of all these writings for American Reconstruction were self-evident.[6]

Not surprisingly, white southerners drew rather different conclusions from the West Indian example. Opponents of Reconstruction seized upon Morant Bay and the demise of local self-government in the islands to illustrate the dangers of black suffrage and rule by "representatives of hordes of ignorant negroes." Democratic newspapers, north and south, were filled during the early days of Reconstruction with lurid reports of West Indian blacks sinking into a "savage state" when liberated from the controlling influence of whites. In Haiti, supposedly, they had reverted to barbarism, paganism, and even human sacrifice, and, said the New York *World*, "intimations of analogous phenomena have already reached us from the region of the lower Mississippi."[7]

Most important, the West Indies demonstrated that plantations could not be maintained with free labor: "the experiments made in Hayti and Jamaica settled that question long ago." J. D. B. De Bow, the South's foremost economic writer, amassed statistics to demonstrate the collapse of the West Indian economies and the indolence of the blacks. Julius J. Fleming, the South Carolina journalist, noted, "It seems to be a conceded fact that in all countries where slavery has existed and been abolished the great difficulty in the way of improvement has been the very subject of labor." Certainly, the Caribbean example reinforced the conviction that American blacks must be prevented from obtaining access to land: otherwise, they would "add nothing to those products which the world especially needs." If the South were to escape the fate of Caribbean societies, it could only be through "some well regulated system of labor, . . . devised by the white man." The emancipated slave, the Louisville *Democrat* concluded after a survey of the West Indies, needed to be taught that "he is *free*, but free only to labor."[8]

Whatever their ultimate conclusions, contemporaries were not wrong to draw parallels between American and Caribbean emancipations. For when viewed in terms of the response of blacks and whites to the end of slavery, the quest of the former slaves for autonomy and the desire of planters for a disciplined labor force, what is remarkable is the similarity between the American experience and that of other societies. As in the Caribbean and, indeed, everywhere else that plantation slavery was abolished, American emancipation raised the interrelated questions of labor control and access to economic resources. The plantation system never dominated the entire South as it did in the islands, yet both before and after emancipation, it helped define the quality of race relations and the nature of economic enterprise in the region as a whole. It was in the plantation black belt that the majority of the emancipated slaves lived, and it was the necessity, as perceived by whites, of maintaining the plantation system, that made labor such an obsession in the aftermath of emancipation. As Christopher G. Memminger, former Confederate secretary of the treasury, observed in 1865, politics, race relations, and the social consequences of abolition all turned "upon the decision which shall be made upon the mode of organizing the labor of the African race."[9]

As in the Caribbean, American freedmen adopted an interpretation of the implications of emancipation rather different from that of their former masters. Sir Frederick Bruce, the British ambassador to the United States, discerned little difference between the behavior of American and West Indian freedmen: "The negro here seems like his brother in Jamaica, to object to labour for hire, and to desire to become proprietor of his patch of land." The desire for land, sometimes judged "irrational" when viewed simply as a matter of dollars and cents, reflected the recognition that, whatever its limitations, land ownership ensured the freedmen a degree of control over the time and labor of themselves and their families. Candid observers who complained blacks were lazy and shiftless had to admit that there was "one motive sufficiently powerful to break this spell, and that is the *desire to own land*. That will arouse all that is dormant in their natures." Equally a sign of the desire for autonomy was the widespread withdrawal of women from plantation field labor, a phenomenon to which contemporaries attributed a good part of the postwar labor shortage.[10]

For the large majority of blacks who did not fulfill the dream of independence as owners or renters of land, the plantation remained an arena of ongoing conflict. In postemancipation east Africa, according to Frederick Cooper, "the smallest question— whether to plant a clove or cashew nut tree—became questions not just of marginal utility, but of class power." And so it was in the postemancipation South, where disputes over supervision by overseers, direction of the labor of black women and children, and work like repairing fences, ditches, and buildings not directly related to the crop at hand, followed the end of slavery. Emancipation ushered in a period of what that perceptive South Carolina planter William H. Trescot called "the perpetual trouble that belongs to a time of social change."[11]

The eventual solution to the labor problem in the post–Civil War cotton South was the system of sharecropping, which evolved out of an economic struggle in which planters were able to prevent most blacks from gaining access to land, while the freedmen utilized the labor shortage (and in many cases, the assistance of the Freedmen's Bureau) to oppose efforts to put them back to work in conditions, especially gang labor, reminiscent of slavery. A way station between independent farming and wage labor, sharecropping would later become associated with a credit system that reduced many tenants to semipeonage. Yet this later development should not obscure the fact that, in a comparative perspective, sharecropping afforded agricultural laborers more control over their own time, labor, and family arrangements, and more hope of economic advancement, than many other modes of labor organization. Sharecroppers were not "coolie" laborers, not directly supervised wage workers.[12] And whatever its inherent economic logic, large numbers of planters believed sharecropping did not ensure the requisite degree of control over the labor force. Sharecropping, complained one planter, "is wrong policy; it makes the laborer too independent; he becomes a partner, and has a right to be consulted." Such planters preferred a complete transition to capitalist agriculture, with a closely supervised labor force working for wages. A wage system did in fact emerge on Louisiana sugar plantations and many Upper South tobacco farms. But in general, sharecropping became the South's replacement system of labor after the end of slavery. "To no laboring class," said a southern senator, "has capital—land—ever made such concessions as have been made to the colored people at the South."[13]

As in the Caribbean, the form of agrarian class relations that succeeded American slavery resulted from a struggle fought out on the plantations themselves. What made the American experience distinct was that the polity as well as the field became an arena of confrontation between former master and former slave.

Here, emancipation occurred in a republic. In the British Empire, as one historian notes, "the question, 'does a black man equal a white man?' had little meaning in an age when few thought all white men deserved equality." In America, however, where equality before the law was the foundation of the political culture, emancipation led inexorably to demands for civil and political rights for the former slaves. In contrast to Caribbean peasants, moreover, whose major ambition seems to have been to be left alone, Afro-Americans demanded full participation in the political life of the nation. Nowhere else did blacks achieve a comparable degree of political influence after the end of slavery. "Their civil and political elevation," as a Tennessee congressman put it, "is unparalleled in the history of nations. . . . France and England emancipated their slaves, but the emancipated never dreamed that they should have letters of nobility, or should be elevated to the woolsack."[14]

Black suffrage fundamentally altered the terms of the postemancipation conflict in the United States. Far more than in the Caribbean and Africa, where white planters, farmers, and mine owners monopolized local political power, state and local government in America became a battleground between contending social classes, including the black laborer. Southern planters, initially restored to local power during Presidential Reconstruction, sought to use the state to stabilize the plantation system and secure their control of the labor force. With the advent of Radical Reconstruction, the role of the state was transformed and the freedmen won, in the vote, a form of leverage their counterparts in other societies did not possess. Then, after Redemption, political and economic authority once again coincided in the South. If in the long run, planters, like their counterparts elsewhere, largely succeeded in shaping the political economy of emancipation in their own interests, by the same token Radical Reconstruction stands as a unique moment when local political authority actually sought to advance the interests of the black laborer. Many of the specific issues upon which postemancipation southern politics turned were the same as in the Caribbean and Africa: immigration, labor laws, the definition of property rights, taxation, and fiscal policy. The conflict over these questions, and its eventual outcome, reveal how much of postemancipation politics was defined by the "labor problem."

As in the Caribbean, some American planters advocated in the aftermath of emancipation that the government directly promote "the accumulation of population," to break the bargaining power of black labor. Immigration, said one observer, would solve two problems at once: "If you would control [the freedman's] political power, you must outvote him; and if you would control him as a laborer, you must fill the country with a more congenial and more reliable laborer."[15]

Many southern states established agencies after the Civil War to encourage immigration from Europe, but the results were disappointing. Of the millions of immigrants landing in New York, Boston, and other northern cities, only a handful made their way south, a reflection, in part, of the ambivalent attitude white southerners communicated about their desire for immigration in the first place. Some reformers looked upon immigrants as prospective landholders; they urged planters to break up the large estates and make land available on easy terms to newcomers. Generally, however, immigration was intended not to undermine the plantation system, but to preserve it. A Republican newspaper was not incorrect when it concluded that the appeal for immigration, "when stripped of its verbosity, is about as follows: 'We have lands but can no longer control the niggers; . . . hence we want Northern laborers, Irish laborers, German laborers, to come down and take their places, to work our lands for ten dollars a month and rations of cornmeal and bacon.'"[16]

"Immigration," a prominent North Carolina lawyer wrote in 1865, "would, doubtless, be a blessing to us, provided we could always control it, and make it entirely subservient to our wants." As in the Caribbean, many planters concluded that indentured laborers would admirably meet this need. West Indian experiments with "coolie" labor were widely publicized in the post–Civil War southern press, and Chinese contract laborers were known to be at work in mines, railroad construction, and large-scale agriculture in contemporary California. A commercial agency offered to deliver "coolies" under five-to-seven-year contracts to Mississippi planters in 1865, and two years later a few Chinese, dispatched from Cuba by southerners living there, arrived to labor in Louisiana sugar fields. Robert Somers, the traveling British correspondent, encountered a gang of some six hundred Chinese laborers, drawn from California, at work on the Alabama and Chattanooga Railroad in 1871; and a number of Chinese laborers were introduced into the Yazoo-Mississippi delta around the same time. But despite enthusiastic predictions of how the Chinese would transform the labor situation (a Kentucky newspaper declared that with the coming of the Chinese, "the tune . . . will not be 'forty acres and a mule,' but . . . 'work nigger or starve'"), the total number of Chinese in the South never exceeded a handful. And many who were introduced proved less docile than anticipated, abandoning plantation labor to set up as small-scale merchants and truck farmers.[17]

Compared with the situation in Trinidad and British Guiana, the need for imported laborers was less in the United States, and the obstacles to their introduction greater. Relatively few blacks had been able to abandon the plantations to take up independent farming. There was also the danger that meddling northerners would bestow the vote on the Chinese, further exacerbating political problems in the Reconstruction South. Blacks, moreover, exercising a measure of political power during Reconstruction, opposed the introduction of "coolies." And federal authorities warned that any effort to bring in laborers under long-term indentures would be deemed a violation of the 1862 statute outlawing the "Coolie Trade." During Reconstruction, Commissioner of Immigration A. N. Congar and Secretary of the Treasury George S. Boutwell promised that "all vigilance" would be exercised to suppress "this new modification of the slave trade."[18]

As in the Caribbean, the effort to introduce Chinese labor in the postbellum South formed only one part of a broader effort to use the power of the state to shape the postemancipation economic order and create a dependent plantation labor force. "There must be stringent laws to control the negroes, and require them to fulfill their contracts of labor on the farms," wrote a South Carolina planter in 1865. "No one will venture to engage in agricultural occupations without some guarantee that his labor is to be controlled and continued under penalties and forfeitures." While a few Bourbons dreamt of compensation for their slave property or even a Supreme Court challenge to the Emancipation Proclamation, most southern whites accepted the fact that slavery was dead. But its dissolution, many believed, need not mean the demise of the plantation. "I am sure we will not be allowed even to contend for gradual emancipation," wrote Texas political leader and railroad promoter J. W. Throckmorton in August, 1865. "But I do believe we will be enabled to adopt a coercive system of labor."[19]

The outcome of such pressures was the Black Codes of 1865 and 1866. Ostensibly, their purpose was to outline the legal rights to be enjoyed by the former slaves. Generally, blacks were accorded the right to acquire and own property, marry, make contracts, sue and be sued, and testify in court in cases involving persons of their own color. But the main focus of the laws was labor. As a New Orleans newspaper put it, with slavery dead, a new labor system must "be prescribed and enforced by the state."[20]

First to rise to the challenge were the legislatures of Mississippi and South Carolina. The Mississippi Code required all blacks to possess, each January, written evidence of employment for the coming year. Laborers leaving their jobs before the contract expired would forfeit all wages up to that time, and the law empowered every white person to arrest any black who deserted the service of his employer. Any person offering work to a laborer already under contract was liable to a fine of five hundred dollars or a prison sentence. Finally, to ensure that no economic opportunities apart from plantation labor remained for the freedmen, they were forbidden to rent land in rural areas.

A vagrancy statute, enacted at the same time, imposed fines or involuntary labor on a bizarre catalog of antisocial types:

> rogues and vagabonds, idle and dissipated persons, beggars, jugglers, or persons practicing unlawful games or plays, runaways, common drunkards, common night-walkers, lewd, wanton, or lascivious persons, . . . common railers and

brawlers, persons who neglect their calling or employment, misspend what they earn, or do not provide for the support of themselves or their families, or dependents, and all other idle and disorderly persons, including all who neglect all lawful business, habitually misspend their time by frequenting houses of ill-fame, gaming-houses, or tippling shops.

And an apprenticeship law permitted the binding out to white employers of black orphans and children whose parents were unable to support them, with "the former owner of said minors" enjoying "the preferance." In case anything had been overlooked, all previous penal codes defining offences of slaves were declared to remain in force, unless specifically altered by law.

South Carolina's Black Code was, in some respects, even more discriminatory. It did not prohibit blacks from renting land, but barred them from following any occupation other than farmer or servant except by paying an annual tax ranging from ten to one hundred dollars. Blacks were required to sign annual contracts, and there were elaborate provisions regulating such agreements, including labor from sunup to sundown, deductions from wages for time not worked, and a prohibition against leaving the plantation or entertaining guests upon it, without permission. Apprenticeship provisions were extended to black children whose parents "are not teaching them habits of industry and honesty; or are persons of notoriously bad character," and a vagrancy law, even more anachronistic in tone than Mississippi's, applied, among others, to "common gamblers, persons who lead disorderly lives or keep or frequent disorderly or disreputable houses; . . . those who are engaged in representing . . . without license, any tragedy, interlude, comedy, farce, play, . . . exhibition of the circus, sleight of hand, wax-works; . . . fortune tellers, sturdy beggars, common drunkards." The image of bands of black thespians undermining plantation discipline by presenting unlicensed theatrical productions in South Carolina truly boggles the imagination.[21]

The uproar created by this legislation led other southern states to modify the language and provisions, if not the underlying intention, of early legislation regarding freedmen. Vir-

tually all the former Confederate states enacted sweeping vagrancy, apprenticeship, labor contract, and antienticement
legislation. Florida's code, drawn up by a three-member commission whose report praised slavery as a "benign" institution
whose only shortcoming was its inadequate regulation of black
sexual behavior, made disobedience, impudence, or even "dis-
respect" to the employer a crime. Louisiana and Texas, seeking
to counteract the withdrawal of black women from field labor,
declared that labor contracts "shall embrace the labor of all the
members of the family able to work." Apprenticeship laws continued to seize upon the consequences of slavery—the separation of families and the poverty of the freedmen—as the excuse
for securing to planters the labor of black minors free of expense.
Many localities supplemented these measures with vagrancy ordinances of their own.[22]

The laws of the southern states concerning labor, *De Bow's
Review* claimed in 1866, were as "liberal, generous, and altogether as humane and equitable as the legislation of any country in the world under similar circumstances." De Bow was not
being entirely disingenuous, for despite their excesses, the Black
Codes were not as severe as the *Code Rural* of Haiti or some of
the statutes enacted in the British Caribbean after emancipation. Southerners, indeed, insisted that precedents existed even
in free labor societies for strict legal regulation of the labor force.
"We have been informed by a distinguished jurist, who is a
member elect of the Virginia Legislature," reported a South Carolina newspaper, "that the 'labor laws' of England . . . contain
just such provisions for the protection of the employer as are
now needed . . . at the South." And, it is true, laws subjecting
employees, but not employers, to criminal penalties for breach
of contract remained on the British statute books until 1875,
and were widely enforced. Draconian English vagrancy laws,
however, had long since fallen into abeyance. As the constitutional scholar Charles Fairman observes, vagrancy laws exist
everywhere, but are generally "allowed to slumber out of sight."
What is critical is the manner of their enforcement, and in the
South of 1865 and 1866, with judicial and police authority in the
hands of the planter class and its friends, impartial administra-

tion was an impossibility. Many southern vagrancy laws, in fact, contained no reference to race. But as John W. DuBose, the Alabama planter and Democratic politico later remarked, "the vagrant contemplated was the plantation negro."[23]

The Black Codes are worth dwelling upon not because of any long-range practical effect—most provisions were quickly voided by the army or Freedmen's Bureau, or invalidated by the Civil Rights Act of 1866—but because of their immediate political impact and what they reveal about the likely shape of southern economic relations if left to the undisputed control of the planters. As W. E. B. Du Bois observed, the Codes represented "what the South proposed to do to the emancipated Negro, unless restrained by the nation." The Codes persuaded many in the North that continuing federal intervention was essential if the fundamental rights of the freedmen were to be protected. They convinced southern blacks as well that their former owners could not be entrusted with political power. The "undisputed history" of Presidential Reconstruction, black Congressman Josiah Walls later recalled, explained why southern blacks refused to cast Democratic ballots, and stood as a warning "as to what they will do if they should again obtain control of this Government." But, as quickly as planters attempted to call forth the power of the state in their own interests, their political hegemony was swept away, and a new series of measures regarding labor was placed on the southern statute books.[24]

Radical Reconstruction, in this respect, profoundly if temporarily affected the relationship of the state to the economic order. The remnants of the Black Codes were repealed and laws were passed seeking to protect blacks from arbitrary dismissal and to ensure payment for time worked. "There is a law now in this State," a black state senator from Florida told a congressional committee, "that allows a man to get what he works for." By the same token, planters' pleas for legislation "the more effectually to secure punctually the observance and performance of labor contracts" went unheeded. Ironically, even those few blacks who managed to acquire land began to complain that the law gave them no assistance in regulating hired labor. One wrote Mississippi's Governor Adelbert Ames that his hands had left to work for a white farmer, "and no man can make a cotton crop that way. Had ought to be made to stay all the year till the crop is gathered. . . . The smart working folks can't live any longer without some laws to fix things up."[25]

The tenor of Reconstruction legislation concerning labor was summed up in a complaint by a South Carolina agricultural journal: "Under the laws of most of the Southern States ample protection is afforded to tenants and very little to landlords." Equally important, the machinery of justice had, particularly in the black belt, been wrested from the planter class. As blacks and their white Republican allies took control of local courts, sheriff's offices, and justiceships of the peace, there were increasing complaints that vagrancy laws went unenforced, trespass was left unpunished, and efforts to discipline troublesome laborers enjoyed no support from the state. "By the law of the State," one planter declared in 1872, "you cannot dismiss from your plantation this intolerable nuisance [a laborer who would not work] after he has made a contract with you, until the year closes. If you take him to a Trial Justice, it costs you five to ten dollars, and the delinquent is ordered to do better, which he never does." A Mississippi observer agreed: "It is clearly demonstrative that negro labor is not reliable, especially as the negro is now a politician and office holder."[26]

With Redemption, the state again stepped forward as an instrument of labor control. Georgia's Redeemer Governor James M. Smith was quite candid about the intention: "We may hold inviolate every law of the United States, and still so legislate upon our labor system as to retain our old plantation system." The writings of William Cohen, Pete Daniel, and others have illuminated the complex system of legal controls intended to secure a dependent labor force in the Redeemer South. Not all these measures, of course, were entirely effective. Black efforts to escape the clutches of tenancy and debt peonage persisted, and federal law placed limits on measures forthrightly designed to restrain the freedmen's mobility. The point is not that the law succeeded fully in its aims, but that the state's intervention altered the balance of economic power between black and white.[27]

What one black political leader called "the class legislation of the Democrats against the race" embraced vagrancy laws, restrictions on labor agents, laws against "enticing" a worker to leave his employment, and criminal penalties for breach of contract. Apart from a few remaining enclaves of black political power, moreover, these laws were now administered by white sheriffs and judges who owed no political debt to the black community. Such legislation, as a Tennessee black convention noted in 1875, was calculated "to make personal liberty an utter impossibility, and . . . place the race in a condition of servitude scarcely less degrading than that endured before the late civil war." As required by the Fourteenth Amendment, the statutes were, on the surface, color-blind—in this respect they differed from the Black Codes of Presidential Reconstruction. But as the Tennessee blacks commented, "a single instance of punishment of whites under these acts has never occurred, and is not expected."[28]

Legislation attempting to limit the mobility of black laborers was, however, only one instance of the use of the law to affect the new class relations resulting from emancipation. In recent years significant studies by both legal and economic historians have detailed the law's relationship to economic change and the ways the courts act to define and redefine property rights. Morton Horwitz, for example, has detailed how, in the antebellum North, a society undergoing a rapid expansion of capitalist economic relations, the law moved from protecting one form of property—that of small, independent owners—to enhancing the property rights of corporations, while increasingly treating labor as a commodity like any other in the marketplace. An analogous legal transformation occurred in the postemancipation South. The abolition of slavery entailed not simply an adjustment to the demise of one species of property, but a redefinition of property rights in general. Here, the law had a decisive role to play.

As Mr. Justice Jackson once observed, "Only those economic advantages are 'rights' which have the law back of them." The market itself is defined and sanctified by law, depending for its existence upon a set of legally defined codes of permissible behavior. Rights to property are, in the end, delimited by the law, and in the United States, as elsewhere, abolition threw open to question the legitimacy of planters' control of property other than slaves.[29]

As far as most southern whites were concerned, the issue of property rights for the former slaves simply did not arise. As General Robert V. Richardson put it in 1865, "The emancipated slaves own nothing, because nothing but freedom has been given to them."[30] Blacks, on the other hand, contended that freedom should carry with it a stake in the soil, a demand reminiscent of the aspirations of Caribbean freedmen, but legitimized in ways distinctively American.

Blacks in the Caribbean, as we have seen, had enjoyed under slavery the "right" to extensive provision grounds, the embryo of the postemancipation peasantry. Many American slaveholders also permitted blacks to keep chickens and sometimes hogs, to raise vegetables to supplement their diets, and to sell the products of their "kitchen gardens" to raise spending money. Slaves, Eugene D. Genovese contends, came to view these gardens as a right rather than a privilege, but they were far less extensive than their counterparts in the West Indies, and American slaves tended to market their corn, eggs, vegetables, and pork directly to the planter rather than at town markets as in Jamaica. Only in coastal Georgia and South Carolina, where the task system allowed slaves considerable time to cultivate their own crops and the planters were absent for much of the year, did an extensive system of marketing and property accumulation emerge under American slavery.[31]

Blacks' claim to landed property in the aftermath of American emancipation, then, was not primarily legitimized as a "right" that had been recognized during bondage. Rather, it rested on a claim to compensation for their unrequited toil as slaves. It was a common misconception among southern whites that, for blacks, freedom meant an escape from all labor. Actually, as a group of black ministers explained to Secretary of War Edwin Stanton in their famous Savannah "Colloquy," blacks understood by slavery not toil, but unrequited toil, and freedom they defined as "placing us where we could reap the fruit of our own labor."

As Lincoln had emphasized so persuasively over the years,

slavery was a standing repudiation of the right of the working-man to the fruits of his labor. To blacks the justice of a claim to land based on unrequited labor seemed self-evident. It was not that blacks challenged the notion of private property per se; rather, they viewed the accumulated property of the planters as having been illegitimately acquired. Eliphalet Whittlesey, former commander of black troops and North Carolina Freedmen's Bureau assistant commissioner, explained the distinction to a congressional committee, when asked whether blacks generally understood what is meant by property: "Yes, sir; so far as their relations to strangers, to northern men, and to neighbors is concerned; but they have an idea that they have a certain right to the property of their former masters, that they have earned it, and that if they can lay their hands on any of it, it is so much that belongs to them." Or, as an Alabama black convention resolved, "The property which they hold was nearly all earned by the sweat of *our* brows."[32]

In its most sophisticated form, this claim to land rested on an appreciation of the role blacks had historically played in the evolution of the American economy. This was the import of the remarkable speech delivered by freedman Bayley Wyat protesting the eviction of blacks from a contraband camp in Virginia in 1866:

> We has a right to the land where we are located. For why? I tell you. Our wives, our children, our husbands, has been sold over and over again to purchase the lands we now locates upon; for that reason we have a divine right to the land. . . . And den didn't we clear the land, and raise de crops ob corn, ob cotton, ob tobacco, ob rice, ob sugar, ob everything. And den didn't dem large cities in de North grow up on de cotton and de sugars and de rice dat we made? . . . I say dey has grown rich, and my people is poor.

Such an appeal, Georgia lawyer Elias Yulee responded, was "mere nonsense." As he informed Georgia blacks in 1868, "as well may the Irish laborer claim New York city, because by his labor all the stores and residences there were constructed. Or claim our railroads because they labored on them with their shovels and wheelbarrows."[33]

Yulee's comment illuminates the paradoxical double quality of free labor. As Marx emphasized, free labor is not bound as serf or slave, but is also "free" in that it enjoys no claim to the means of production. As labor became free, E. P. Thompson has explained in a different context, so "labour's product came to be seen as something totally distinct, the property of landowner or employee." Emancipation thus demanded a sharper demarcation between property and labor than had existed under slavery (since the laborer himself was no longer property). And, while the distribution of land never did materialize, the conflict over the definition of property rights continued on many fronts in the postbellum South. For the system of property rights formed an essential part of the social framework within which the postemancipation "labor problem" was worked out.

Like their Caribbean counterparts, southern freedmen did not believe the end of slavery should mean a diminution of either the privileges or level of income they had enjoyed as slaves. The slave, after all, possessed one customary "right" no free laborer could claim—the right to subsistence. Henry Lee Higginson, Harvard graduate and Civil War veteran who with his wife and two friends purchased a Georgia plantation in 1865, found the freedmen did not "understand the value of work and wages" in the same manner as northern workers. "They think," Mrs. Higginson observed, "they ought to get all their living and have wages besides, all extra."[34]

The "right" to subsistence, however, had no place in a free labor society. Indeed, the end of slavery required a complete overhaul of the law; in a wide variety of instances, what had once been "rights" were now redefined as crimes. Under slavery theft of food belonging to the owner had been all but universal. Virtually every planter complained of the killing of poultry and hogs, and the plundering of corn cribs, smoke houses, and kitchens by the slaves. Most planters seem to have taken a lenient attitude, particularly where the theft was for purposes of consumption (selling stolen food was another matter entirely). "I do not think a man ever prosecuted his own slave for a larceny," a South Carolina lawyer remarked after the Civil War. Most masters seem to have assumed that thievery was simply another of those inborn black traits that made slavery necessary in the first place. To slaves, on the other hand, as one freedman later recalled, theft simply followed the Biblical injunction: "Where ye labor there shall ye reap."[35]

Under slavery the boundary between public and private authority had been indefinite; crimes like theft, looked upon as labor troubles, were generally settled by planters themselves. Abolition obviously required a restructuring and strengthening of the enforcement machinery. As George A. Trenholm, a prominent South Carolina merchant, explained soon after the end of the Civil War, "Hitherto these depredations were either overlooked, or the culprit punished lightly and restored to favor. Now it must necessarily be different. Theft is no longer an offense against his master, but a crime against the State." Thus, in the transition from slavery to freedom, the criminal law emerged as a means of enforcing the property rights and demands for labor discipline of the landowner against the claims of the former slave.

Everywhere, the end of slavery witnessed a determined effort to put down larceny by the former slaves. In the United States as well, planters complained of the widespread depredations committed by the freedmen. No one was able to raise stock in South Carolina, according to one planter, because "the negroes have shot and stolen them all." In Louisiana the "thefts of animals by the 'colored gentlemen' who do not want to work," were described in 1868 as "appalling." Some blacks forthrightly contended that, as under slavery, they had a "right" to steal from whites. One North Carolina preacher imprisoned for larceny, had been "known to say from his pulpit that it was no harm to steal from white people, that his hearers would only be getting back what belonged to them." Others, including some white observers, interpreted theft as a form of retaliation against inequitable labor practices. A Freedmen's Bureau agent explained that during Presidential Reconstruction, with planters in control of local courts, the only recourse of blacks driven from plantations without the compensation due them was "to steal and to kill the stock of the planter who defrauds him."[36]

Where blacks or their white allies achieved local political

power during Reconstruction, planters contended that laws against theft went unenforced. "Let him know that if he steals for a living, as he now does, he will not be tried by a scallawag judge, nor a negro jury," one planter insisted. Another echoed, "We have negro magistrates, and negro jurymen, and we cannot convict the thieves." Black justices of the peace were said not to punish the theft of livestock and seed cotton by blacks, and as for black jurors, they "had a strong predilection for their own race, and they were not very clear in their ideas of the difference between right and wrong." Or, to put it more accurately, their sense of right and wrong differed from that of their former owners.[37]

With Redemption came a concerted legal offensive "for the protection of the cotton planters." Measures such as sunset laws, meant to discourage theft by prohibiting the sale of seed cotton and sometimes all farm products between sundown and sunup, had been regularly proposed and just as regularly rejected during Reconstruction. Now they were placed on the statute books. To circumvent the Fourteenth Amendment and federal civil rights laws, such measures did not mention blacks specifically, but often applied only to counties with black majorities. Alabama made the sale of seed cotton to a merchant at any time of the day or night a felony in nine black belt counties. Such laws not only reinforced the property rights of the planters, but undermined those of the former slaves, limiting the economic alternatives available to them. As Alabama black leader James T. Rapier explained, "If a man commits a crime he ought to be punished, but every man ought to have a right to dispose of his own property. . . . I may raise as much cotton as I please in the seed, but I am prohibited by law from selling it to anybody but the landlord."[38]

At the same time, the southern criminal law was transformed to increase sharply the penalty for petty theft (and provide a source of involuntary labor for those leasing convicts from the state). There was precedent for such measures in the early Black Codes. South Carolina's criminal law as amended in 1865 had been, a southern writer noted, "emphatically a bloody code." It made every theft a felony punishable by death, the result of which, critics charged, was that convictions would be impossible to obtain. Severe criminal penalties for theft fell into abeyance during Reconstruction, but were revived by the Redeemers. South Carolina did not go to quite the extreme of 1865, but did increase the penalty for the theft of any livestock to a fine of up to one thousand dollars and a maximum of ten years in prison. In North Carolina and Virginia after Reconstruction, a black spokesman charged, "They send him to the penitentiary if he steals a chicken." Mississippi, in its famous "pig law," defined the theft of any cattle or swine as grand larceny, punishable by five years in prison. The criminal laws of Mississippi, a federal official remarked, "appear to me to be a shame to the manhood of the state."[39]

Such legislation made the convict lease system, which had originated on a small scale during Reconstruction, a lucrative business in the Redeemer South. Republicans were not far wrong when they charged of the system in Texas, "The courts of law are employed to re-enslave the colored race." Another result was that blacks, who had looked to the state for protection during Reconstruction, now correctly viewed it as simply an instrument of class rule. There was no rational correspondence between crime and punishment, blacks were excluded from judgeships and jury service in most of the South, and black sheriffs and policemen, stunning innovations of Reconstruction, were removed from their positions. In these circumstances the law could hardly fulfill a "hegemonic" function—providing a seemingly disinterested standard of justice independent of the authority of any particular social class. Conviction of crime in such a legal order carried little onus in the black community, indeed it sometimes was associated with a kind of heroism or notoriety. In the courts of Presidential Reconstruction, a petition of Charleston blacks had complained in early 1867, "Justice is mocked and injustice is clothed in the garb of righteousness." The same was true of the legal order fashioned by the Redeemers.[40]

A further example of the use of law to redefine class and property relations and enhance labor discipline is the evolution of legislation concerning liens and the control of standing crops.

Crop liens as a form of agricultural credit had originated soon after the Civil War, but the early statutes made no distinction among suppliers—anyone who made advances could hold a lien on the crop. The Freedmen's Bureau and some military officials superimposed upon the credit system the requirement that laborers enjoy a lien superior to all others for their wages or share of the crop, and several states during Reconstruction enacted the laborer's lien into law. Some went further and prohibited the removal of crops from a plantation until the division and settlement took place before some disinterested party. As a result, control of the crop was somewhat indeterminate during Reconstruction.[41]

As in so many other areas, what was an open question, an arena of conflict during Reconstruction, became a closed issue with Redemption. The right to property and the terms of credit —the essence of economic power in the rural South—were redefined in the interest of the planter. Generally, landlords were awarded a lien superior to that of the laborer for wages or merchants for supplies. North Carolina placed the entire crop in the hands of the landlord until rent was fully paid, and allowed no challenge to his decision as to when the tenant's obligation had been fulfilled. In Texas the law prohibited the tenant from selling anything until the landlord received his rent. The law attempted to accomplish what planters by themselves had failed to achieve: the complete separation of the freedmen from the means of production, the creation of a true agricultural proletariat. Beginning with *Appling* v. *Odum* in Georgia in 1872, a series of court decisions defined the sharecropper simply as a wage worker, with no control of the land during the term of his lease, and no right to a portion of the crop until division. Croppers, said the court, enjoyed "no possession of the premises, . . . only a right to go on the land to plant, work, and gather the crop."[42]

Conflicts over the legal definition of contract rights, liens and tenancy are familiar legacies of emancipation. Less well known, although equally important as an example of the reshaping of property relations, was the matter of fencing, an explosive political issue in parts of the postemancipation South because it directly involved the laborer's access to economic resources and alternative means of subsistence.

There is no more compelling symbol of private property than a fence. In his *Discourse on the Origin of Inequality*, Rousseau identified as "the real founder of civil society," the first man who enclosed a piece of land. (He also blamed this mythical personage for all the "crimes, wars and murders, . . . horrors and misfortunes" which resulted from private ownership of "the fruits of the earth.") The antebellum South, a society in which social relations were in some ways still precapitalist, also seems to have been less than completely committed to the private appropriation of land. The common law doctrine requiring that livestock be confined to the property of its owner, as in New England, did not apply in the slave states. Rather, the farmer, not the stockowner, was required to fence in his holdings. All unenclosed land, even if privately owned, in effect became public commons, on which anyone could graze his livestock.

"Progressive planters" frequently voiced dissatisfaction over the expense of fencing and the damage caused by livestock roaming on their lands. The law allowed the landless and small property-holders to graze livestock, sometimes even large herds, on the lands of their wealthy neighbors. In the late antebellum period, a few states took the first steps toward requiring stockowners to fence in their animals. But, as one planter commented, "the right of common" was so deeply ingrained that it was "out of the power of any farmer in this county to enclose a standing pasture." Property rights, Edmund Ruffin lamented, were simply not appreciated as thoroughly in the slave states as in the North.[43]

Disputes over fencing were by no means confined to the South in nineteenth-century America. A Midwestern agricultural magazine in the 1840s spoke of "brutal conflicts" over damages done by animals running at large, and there were persistent battles on the Iowa and Illinois prairies between livestock men and farmers. By the 1870s, advocates of stock confinement had achieved their legislative aims in the Midwest. Simultaneously, California required cattlemen to fence in their animals in the rich agricultural region of the San Joaquin Valley, and a similar battle raged on the Texas prairies between cattle barons using barbed wire to enclose public lands, and small farmers rallying under the banner of "free grass."[44]

In the South, emancipation added a new entry to the list of combatants: the freedmen. Blacks, it appears, had a vested interest in existing southern fence laws, which allowed landless freedmen to own animals, grazing them on the property of others. The free ranging of livestock also facilitated the stealing and slaughtering of hogs by blacks, of which so many white farmers complained. The northern journalist and liberal reformer Charles Nordhoff was appalled by the southern practice of "letting animals run half wild in the woods." It was unrealistic, he believed, to expect blacks to "respect property rights so loosely asserted."

A chorus of complaints was raised during Reconstruction against what one planter termed "the infamous, and barbarous fence laws." Those who believed the climate and lands of the South ideally suited for stock raising, and that a shift to livestock would reduce dependence on black labor, found the fence laws an insuperable obstacle. Railroad companies joined planters in pressing for an end to the open range, since juries often awarded damages to persons whose stock was killed by passing trains. A Mississippi planter summed up the situation: "It is . . . the first duty of every intelligent landowner to arouse himself and keep this subject agitated until we have a law passed."[45]

Even among whites, however, there was strong opposition to such demands. A change in the fence law, the Selma *Southern Argus* explained, "is opposed to the immemorial custom of the country, and encounters the prejudices and arouses the opposition of perhaps a majority of the farmers and planters . . . it is revolutionary in its character, and its enactment into law at this time, and enforcement, would fill the land with dissentions." The *Southern Argus* was concerned about dissentions among whites, not blacks, for yeoman farmers had long cherished the right to let their stock run free on the land of others. But the advent of black suffrage brought to the political arena a group equally adamant in opposing new fence laws. "Even before the recent changes in our government," one agricultural reformer noted in 1873, "the proposition to fence stock met with little favor from the unintelligent masses and now that the suffrage has been so thoroughly debased, it is not likely that Legislative action will abate the evil." Blacks, after all, were generally propertyless, but many owned an animal or two. The open range was essential to enable them to graze their livestock. "All they need," said one writer, "is a little to plant, their diminutive gangs of stock can herd it about over the woods, and are no expense to them." Some freedmen, like the father of Nate Shaw, the protagonist of that classic of oral history, *All God's Dangers*, were able to subsist for a time entirely by hunting and the free ranging of their hogs, thereby avoiding wage labor altogether.[46]

The first tentative steps to close the southern range had been taken during Presidential Reconstruction, directed at the black belt counties where most freedmen lived. Nothing more was done during Reconstruction, but with Redemption the legal offensive resumed. First to act was Georgia, whose Democratic legislature in 1872 passed a law allowing fifty freeholders in any county to petition for a local election on changing the fence laws. Alabama and Mississippi authorized similar elections in the 1880s. Generally, the battle was fought out first in the black counties, although early efforts to enact local statutes were often defeated by the votes of black tenants and laborers. But fraud, state laws restricting the vote on fence issues to landowners, and statutes simply ending common rights in black counties without a popular vote, succeeded by the mid-eighties in enclosing most of the black belt, a severe blow to the ability of freedmen to earn a living independent of plantation labor. The conflict then shifted to the white upcountry, where bitter struggles were waged between agricultural reformers and poorer yeomen determined to preserve their customary rights. The closing of the open range was a long-drawn-out process; in some states it was not completed until well into the twentieth century. But, as with the analogous English enclosure movement of the eighteenth century, the result was a fundamental redefinition of property rights. Southern small farmers and tenants, black and white alike, might well echo the lament of the English rural laborer who had seen his access to the land legislated out of existence: "Parliament may be tender of property; all I know is I had a cow, and an Act of Parliament has taken it from me."[47]

Much the same demise of customary rights allowing an alternative to plantation labor was reflected in another postwar development, the growth of laws to prohibit hunting and fishing on private property. Here, too, the pattern had been established in eighteenth-century England, where a series of game laws, including the infamous Black Act of 1723 making the hunting or stealing of deer and hares in royal forests capital crimes, redefined traditional practices as criminal offenses. Such laws were resented by those accustomed to hunt on privately owned land, and supported by large landowners who saw them as a means of counteracting the inclination to idleness among the poor, as well as preserving a much-esteemed sport.[48]

In the pre-Civil War South, a sparsely settled region whose extensive woods harbored plentiful supplies of game, there were few restrictions on hunting and fishing by free men. Evidence suggests that a significant number of slaves also had experience hunting, trapping game, and fishing. Toward the end of the antebellum period, planters in some counties, fearing the depletion of game for purposes of sport, began to press for the passage of laws to limit the times of year during which hunting could take place, and for stronger penalties against trespass. A handful of such measures was enacted, particularly in the Upper South, but generally their impact was quite limited.[49]

Emancipation did not affect the abundance of the southern streams and forests, but it did transform the social implications of hunting and fishing. Henry Crydenwise, a northern army veteran who worked as overseer on a Mississippi plantation in 1866, was astonished at the profusion and variety of creatures near the plantation. There were bears, panthers, and wildcats, as well as "a large variety of other less dangerous animals," and blacks found in hunting a convenient way of supplementing their meager incomes. For the same reason, planters now agitated for restrictive legislation. "In England and France [they] have to get permits to carry guns as well as to shoot game on their neighbors' premises," wrote a North Carolinian, "but here in this ultra civilized country gangs of negroes prowling the roads and woods nearly every day the most of them with double barrel guns . . . have . . . effectually destroyed the game." In Mississippi, a white woman, apologizing for intruding into the male domain of politics, urged the legislature to "pass the English game laws . . . the laws that old England found necessary, to protect her landed interest from the depredations of white laborers, and then a negro could not have the excuse when seen hunting on other persons estates, that he was only hunting bear, deer, squirrels, birds, etc."[50]

Presidential Reconstruction witnessed legislative efforts to restrict blacks' right to hunt and fish. The Black Codes of several states made it illegal to carry firearms on the premises of any plantation without the permission of the owner, defined hunting or fishing on private property as vagrancy, and imposed taxes on dogs and guns owned by blacks. Georgia in 1866 outlawed hunting on Sundays in counties with large black populations, and forbade the taking of timber, berries, fruit, or anything "of any value whatever" from private property, whether or not fenced. During Reconstruction these laws were repealed or went unenforced, while planter petitions for new trespass and game laws were ignored. "We must have less freedom and more protection to property," said a speaker at the Mississippi State Grange in 1874. "We want something like the anti-dog and anti-gun laws of 1865 and 1866." But, as a visitor to South Carolina explained, so long as the "white man is so poorly represented in the Legislature, the poacher wanders unreproved." Nearly all black families, it seemed, owned shotguns which, as Cyrus Abram, an Alabama freedman, put it, were "a heap of service in shooting squirrels, birds, ducks, and turkeys, etc. That is the way we get a good portion of our meat." In the 1874 election campaign, however, armed whites confiscated the guns belonging to Abram and other freedmen. "My gun was a mighty loss to me," he told a congressional committee, "because it is so hard for a black man to get something to eat."[51]

In the Redeemer period, scores of local ordinances and many state-wide measures were enacted, designed to secure white private property from trespass, thereby discouraging men like Abram from getting "something to eat" without plantation labor. Georgia once again took the lead, restricting hunting and fishing in black belt counties, establishing hunting seasons for deer and fowl, and limiting the ownership of dogs. As in the case of fence laws, the redefinition of private property at the expense of customary rights provoked dissention, especially in white up-country counties where the right to vote could not be as easily restricted or manipulated as in the black belt. Tennessee's Redeemers, for example, were unable to enact a dog law, because, according to one contemporary, "the dog is radicated in the affections of the mountain counties, and dog laws there beget popular uprisings." But those laws which applied in only the black counties faced weaker opposition, and represented a serious restriction on the opportunities for freedmen to earn an independent living.[52]

In one final area, taxation, the relationship between the state and private property was also transformed after the Civil War. Before the war, landed property in the South had gone virtually untaxed, while levies on slaves, commercial activities, luxuries such as carriages, race horses, and gold watches, and licenses on professions provided the bulk of revenue. The result was that white yeomen paid few taxes—their tools, livestock, and personal property were generally exempted—while planters bore a larger burden, but hardly one commensurate with their wealth and income. The tax on slaves and luxury items drew money from the planter class, but the extremely low rate on real estate and the widespread practice of allowing the owner to determine the assessed value of his own land, meant planters could engross large holdings of unimproved land without incurring an added tax burden. During the 1850s, several states moved toward a uniform levy on the value of all property, a simplified and more modern system that had the effect of lessening the burden of urban and commercial interests and increasing the share of rural property holders.[53]

With emancipation, the southern tax system became a battleground where the competing claims of planter and freedman, as well as yeoman farmers and commercial interests, were fought out. In Presidential Reconstruction, planters, like their counterparts in other parts of the world, looked to taxation as one means of compelling blacks to offer their services in the labor market. Less well known than the Black Codes, the revenue laws of 1865 and 1866 formed part of the same overall attempt to create a dependent labor force. While taxes on landed property remained absurdly low (one-tenth of one percent in Mississippi, for example), heavy poll taxes were levied on freedmen, as well as imposts on the earnings of urban craftsmen. Because so much state revenue derived from taxes on individuals, an inequitable situation existed in which "the man with his two thousand acres paid less tax than any one of the scores of hands he may have had in his employ who owned not a dollar's worth of property." Not surprisingly, blacks resented a revenue system whose incidence was unfair, and from whose proceeds, as a North Carolina Freedmen's Bureau agent reported, "they state, and with truth, that they derive no benefit whatever."[54]

Reconstruction witnessed a fundamental restructuring of the southern tax system and the emergence of the level and incidence of taxation as Democratic rallying cries second only to white supremacy. The need to rebuild and expand the social and economic infrastructure of the South, coupled with the sudden growth of the citizenry resulting from emancipation, vastly increased the financial necessities of southern state governments. Moreover, with the fall of property values, tax rates had to rise, simply to produce revenue equivalent to that of the prewar years. But more significant than the overall rate of taxation was the change in its incidence. Every southern state adopted an ad valorem tax on landed and personal property, shifting the burden of taxation to property holders. The result was that planters and poorer white farmers, many for the first time, paid a significant portion of their income as taxes, while propertyless blacks escaped almost scot-free. Democrats complained that apart from poll taxes, blacks contributed nothing to the support of the state, since generally a certain amount of personal property, tools, and livestock was exempted from the new levies. In retrospect, the antebellum years seemed to whites a golden age. As one farmer declared, when asked if his tax of four dollars on one hundred acres of land seemed excessive, "It appears so, sir, to what it was formerly, . . . next to nothing."[55]

In essentially self-sufficient areas like western North Carolina, where "the family do not see as much as $20 in money all the year," even a few dollars tax was a grievous economic burden. "You can not have an idea how destitute of money the country is," a letter from upcountry South Carolina to Governor Robert M. Scott reported in 1871. "The taxes now are the cause of the greatest anxiety and to meet them, people are selling every egg and chicken they can get." Those blacks who managed to acquire property also felt the impact. On the South Carolina Sea Islands, black landowners in 1869 were said to be selling corn, chickens, and pigs to pay a tax amounting to a few dollars. "They stripped their little farms," wrote a northern teacher. Not a few blacks who acquired land in the Reconstruction South subsequently lost it at tax sales, and returned to the plantation labor force. The outcome was indeed ironic. In the Caribbean and southern Africa, taxation was consciously devised to help create a labor force for white plantations, farms, and mines. In American Reconstruction the high taxes needed to finance the school systems, economic improvements, and other measures designed to improve the lot of the freed population sometimes had the unintended result of jeopardizing what economic independence they had achieved.[56]

In some parts of the Reconstruction South, Republican lawmakers designed the tax laws to force land onto the market and stimulate the breakup of the plantation system. "The reformers complain of taxes being too high," said a South Carolina black leader. "I tell you they are not high enough. I want them taxed until they put these lands back where they belong, into the hands of those who worked for them." In this century a progressive land tax, often employed in the Third World, has proved an inefficient means of promoting a redistribution of landed property. The same seems to have been the case during Reconstruction, although the new tax system did seriously inconvenience those holding large tracts of land for purposes of speculation. One result of Reconstruction fiscal policy, it is true, was that vast acreages—one-fifth of the entire area of Mississippi, to cite one example—fell into the hands of the state for nonpayment of taxes. The ultimate disposition of such lands is one of the more fascinating uninvestigated questions of Reconstruction history. State law often required that they be sold at auction in 40-acre plots, and there is some evidence of blacks acquiring land in this manner. The title to such holdings, however, was far from secure, since state laws generally allowed the former owner to redeem his property by paying the back taxes plus a penalty. There was a certain regularity in the way many plantations forfeited for taxes were recovered, forfeited, and recovered again. Such lands continued to be worked by the former owner and tenants, in effect capitalized by a low-interest loan from the state in the form of a delay in tax collection. Where tax auctions did take place, the buyers tended to be neighboring white farmers, land speculators, or urban businessmen, who gathered up considerable expanses at a few cents per acre.[57]

After Redemption, the southern tax system was transformed anew. First of all, the level of taxes was sharply reduced. The parsimony of the Redeemer regimes is notorious; in Louisiana, "they were so economical that public education and other state services to the people almost disappeared." But the reduction in taxes and expenditures did not affect all classes equally. Partly due to upcountry pressure, landed property enjoyed the sharpest decline in tax rates, while privilege and license taxes rose. The reduction in land taxes was not passed along to black tenants. As a black Louisiana politician complained, "The landowners get all the benefit and the laborers none from the reduction in taxes." Reconstruction laws exempting a certain value of property from taxation were replaced by exclusions only for specific items, such as machinery and implements utilized on a plantation. The result was that blacks now paid taxes on virtually every piece of property they owned—tools, mules, even furniture—while larger farmers had several thousand dollars exempted from levy. "The farmer's hoe and plow, and the mechanic's saw and plane," a Georgia Republican newspaper lamented, "must be taxed to support the Government; . . . Show me the rich man who handles a hoe or pushes a plane." Then, too, poll taxes—the most regressive form of revenue—remained in force. The result was that throughout the post-Reconstruction South, as in the postemancipation Caribbean, the poor bore the heaviest burden of taxation and received the fewest public services.[58]

To reiterate the obvious, no one can claim that the complex structure of labor, property, and tax laws initiated immediately after the war, then dismantled during Reconstruction, and finally, with modifications, reinstated after Redemption, were completely successful in controlling the black laborer or shaping the southern economy. The law is an inefficient mechanism for forcing men to work in a disciplined manner, as planters continued to lament long after the end of Reconstruction. Nor could any statute eliminate the colonial status of the South within the national economy, or counteract the slowdown in the rate of growth of world demand for cotton. But the post-Reconstruction legal system did have profound consequences for black and white alike, foreclosing economic possibilities for some, and opening opportunities for others. The issue, as Du Bois noted, was not so much whether the South could produce wealth with free labor—"It was the far more fundamental question of whom this wealth was to belong to and for whose interests laborers were to work."[59]

In poverty, malnutrition, illiteracy, and a host of other burdens, the freedmen paid the highest price for the failure of Reconstruction and the economic stagnation of the plantation South. Even though these hardships were not confined to blacks, the freedmen were caught in a unique web of legal and extralegal coercions which distinguished their plight from that of the growing number of white sharecroppers. To the architects of the post-Reconstruction South, black poverty was a small price to pay for political peace and labor discipline. "I do not think that poverty disturbs their happiness at all," a Georgia editor told a congressional committee. Another Georgian took a slightly different route to the same conclusion: "The Nigger, when poverty stricken . . . will work well for you—but as soon as you get him up and he begins to be prosperous, he becomes impudent and unmanagable." For their part, blacks fully understood that their aspirations were incompatible with those of their former owners. "What motive has he to see you oppressed and down-trodden?" a visiting congressman asked David Graham, an Edgefield County, South Carolina black leader in 1876. "In case I was rich, and all colored men was rich . . . ," Graham replied, "how would he get his labor? He couldn't get it as cheap as he gets it now. . . . His interest is in keeping me poor, so that I will have to hire to some one else."[60]

Here, in the candid recognition of irreconcilable interests, lay a recipe for continuing conflict. And, indeed, it is the ongoing struggle over the definition of freedom and the control of labor that unites the experience of the American South with that of other postemancipation societies. Long after the end of slavery, the conflict would culminate in the enmeshing of blacks in a comprehensive system of segregation, disfranchisement, and, in many cases, virtual peonage, and the proletarianization of the agricultural labor force of the South. Here, as elsewhere, the adjustment to emancipation appears as a saga of persistence rather than change, stagnation rather than progress, the resiliency of an old ruling class rather than the triumph of a new order.

Yet if the ultimate outcome seems in retrospect depressingly similar to the Caribbean and South Africa experiences, by the same token it underscores the uniqueness of Reconstruction in the history of postemancipation societies, and the enduring changes American emancipation did accomplish. However brief its sway, Reconstruction allowed scope for a remarkable political and social mobilization of the black community, opening doors of opportunity that could never again be completely closed. If Reconstruction did not overturn the economic dominance of the planter class, it did prevent the immediate putting into place of a comprehensive legal and judicial system meant to define the political economy of emancipation solely in the planters' interests. Despite Redemption, the complete dispossession and immobilization of the labor force envisioned in 1865 and 1866 never was achieved, and blacks stubbornly clung to the measure of autonomy in day-to-day labor relations assured by sharecropping. Nor were plantation labor controls extended, as in twentieth-century South Africa, into industry, an outcome of great importance when employment opportunities opened for blacks in the North. And Reconstruction established a framework of legal rights enshrined in the Constitution that, while flagrantly violated in practice after Redemption, planted the seeds of future struggle and left intact a vehicle for future federal intervention in southern affairs.

Thus, a subtle dialectic of persistence and change, continuity and conflict, shaped America's adjustment to abolition. As in most other societies that experienced the end of slavery, black aspirations were, in large measure, thwarted and plantation agriculture, in modified form, survived. Yet for a moment, American freedmen had enjoyed an unparalleled opportunity to help shape their own destiny. The legacy of Reconstruction would endure as blacks continued to assert their claims, against unequal odds, to economic autonomy, political citizenship, and a voice in determining the consequences of emancipation.

III

THE EMANCIPATED
WORKER

 In 1876, the final year of Reconstruction, the workers on rice plantations along the Combahee and Ashepoo rivers in South Carolina rose up in a series of strikes. The culmination of more than a decade of labor strife in the rice fields, the contest between the freedmen living on the edge of poverty and the remnant of what had once been the richest portion of the planter class contained all the elements of high drama. "The genius of Dickens," a congressman investigating the affair concluded, "never conceived anything richer or racier than this unvarnished tale of the working people and the planters of South Carolina."[1] Occurring at a time of unprecedented political turmoil in the state, the strikes were quickly overshadowed by the Red Shirt campaign of Wade Hampton and the Democrats, and the final collapse of Reconstruction in the state where its sway had appeared most secure. In histories of the period, they are relegated to little more than a footnote. But the strikes on the Combahee epitomized in microcosm a host of issues central to the legacy of emancipation in the United States: the control of labor, the survival of the plantation, the intimate connection

74

of political authority and economic relations, and the varied means by which the ongoing struggle between former master and former slave was conducted in the aftermath of slavery.

Of the Old South's agricultural staples, none was so constrained by geography as rice. It could be grown with commercial success only along the lower reaches of a few rivers in a coastal belt stretching from the lower Cape Fear of North Carolina to upper Florida. Here the rise and fall of the tides made possible the alternate flooding and draining of the fields essential for rice cultivation. Rice could not be grown too close to the coast, for salt water would destroy the crop, and tidal flows on the upper reaches of the rivers were difficult to regulate, so the plantations clustered at a distance of between five and twenty-five miles from the sea.

"A rice plantation," a visiting journalist observed during Reconstruction, "is, in fact, a huge hydraulic machine, maintained by constant warring against the rivers." The river made cultivation possible, but constantly threatened to destroy the crops. Successful rice growing depended upon an elaborate system of embankments, canals, floodgates, and dikes to coordinate the flooding and draining of the fields, and the slightest leak could ruin the crop. To maintain this elaborate irrigation complex and build expensive threshing mills, rice plantations required investments ranging from $50,000 to $500,000, and large slave populations whose labor in disease-infested swamps was "simple drudgery of the meanest form." Rice was a crop that demanded year-round attention. The seed was generally planted in March, after the soil had been thoroughly prepared. Fields were then flooded, and soon afterwards, drained. After hoeing, they were flooded again, and the procedure was repeated until late August, when harvesting commenced. After the crop had been gathered, there were repairs to be made in the canals and embankments, and then the whole process began again.

The rice kingdom of the late antebellum years encompassed only 100,000 acres. Its epicenter lay in the Georgetown District of South Carolina, which alone produced nearly a third of the nation's crop in 1859. There were also extensive rice plantations on the Cooper River above Charleston, in Beaufort and Colleton

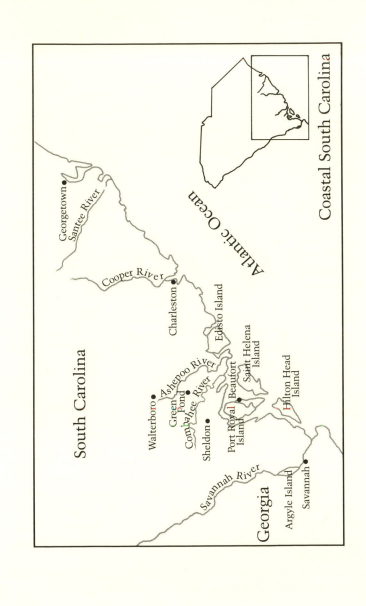

Coastal South Carolina

Districts, South Carolina, and in coastal Georgia. During the 1850s, total rice production had declined as the high price of cotton led some planters to transfer slaves from rice to cotton fields. But Georgia's output increased, as South Carolina planters in search of more fertile lands established plantations along the Savannah River.[2]

Along the rice coast arose one of the most close-knit, aristocratic, and affluent groups of planters in the antebellum South. If ever a set of planters seemed to fit the image of the wealthy grandee, it was the rice aristocracy during its golden age. The most prominent families—the Manigaults, Izards, Allstons, and Heywards—were connected by a web of family and business relations cemented by repeated intermarriages. Most owned several rice plantations; Nathaniel Heyward had acquired no fewer than seventeen on the Combahee, and Robert F. W. Allston seven in the Georgetown region, with a total of six hundred slaves. Few rice aristocrats actually resided on the plantations, preferring to spend their time in luxurious city residences in Charleston, Savannah, Georgetown, or Beaufort, or at country seats in the mountains. Here, surrounded by liveried servants, they pursued their cultural, political, and sporting interests. Immensely rich even for the planter class, they formed a cohesive oligarchy which, in South Carolina, dominated the politics of the low country and, to some extent, the state as a whole. Although they had little direct contact with their numerous slaves, leaving day-to-day management to resident agents, often with a black "headman" directing labor, some rice planters showed a paternalistic concern for the well-being of their human property. Charles Manigault, owner of Gowrie and East Hermitage plantations on Argyle Island in the Savannah River, instructed his overseer when issuing clothing to "send back anything which is not first rate." Yet Manigault also insisted upon a rigid discipline among the slaves, and was not reluctant to sell off troublesome individuals. On their plantations, as in their political and private lives, the rice aristocracy was used to having its own way.[3]

If the rice kingdom gave rise to an exceptional planter aristocracy, so too a distinctive way of life developed among the slaves in the South Carolina and Georgia low country. In cultural autonomy, control over their own time and the pace of work, and even opportunities to acquire property, the slaves on the rice plantations and adjacent Sea Island cotton estates were unique. The extremely high proportion of blacks in the low-country population (85 percent in Georgetown District, 83 percent in Beaufort, and 78 percent in Colleton in 1860) and the importation of large numbers of Africans just before the close of the slave trade in 1808 meant that African culture retained its vitality here to a greater degree than elsewhere in the South. The Gullah dialect distinguished low-country slaves from the rest of the black population. "Those negroes upon the coast are very different from the negroes in Middle and Upper Georgia," General John B. Gordon remarked after the Civil War. "They are almost an entirely different race of people. . . . The negroes have absolutely a language of their own. . . . If a negro were transported . . . to the coast of Georgia, he would not understand at all a great deal that many of the negroes of that coast would say." The "shout," a religious practice of the low-country slaves that reminded Gordon of "the accounts that we have read of the worship of the howling dervishes," also set the region's Afro-American culture apart.[4]

If the vitality of the African inheritance, the Gullah language, and plantations with absentee owners and extremely large black populations all gave the low country a West Indian flavor, the system of labor that developed here was unique. Labor, "the all important item in the well being of a plantation," as one rice planter described it, was organized on the task system. Rather than working in gangs from sunup to sundown, slaves were assigned daily tasks, completion of which left time to cultivate crops of their own, hunt, fish, raise poultry and livestock, or simply enjoy leisure time. The rice plantation, divided into small parcels of land by the irrigation system, was ideally suited to the task system, and it also came to characterize the long-staple cotton plantations nearby. Tasks varied according to the season, but all had long since become standardized, and generally could be completed "with tolerable ease" by most slaves in less than a full day.

For planters, the advantage of the task system was that it drastically reduced the cost of supervising the slaves, while rendering it unnecessary for white planters or overseers to venture very often into the disease-infested low-country swamps. Indeed, the system probably originated because blacks were far less susceptible to yellow fever and malaria than whites, a biological fact that powerfully shaped the social relations of production in colonial South Carolina. For blacks, task organization afforded an unparalleled degree of control over the pace and length of the work day and the opportunity to acquire significant amounts of property. It was not uncommon for low-country slaves to sell crops grown on their own time in Savannah, Beaufort, Georgetown, and Charleston or at nearby country stores, and to acquire horses, cows, household furniture, and even shotguns with the proceeds. Although the task system was premised on the slaves working as individuals, cooperative labor patterns also existed in the rice fields. It was customary for more active hands to assist slower or older ones, and the irrigation process itself required coordination of flooding and draining. Like the "proto-peasantry" of slave Jamaica, low-country blacks had extensive experience managing their own affairs well before emancipation.[5]

The Civil War shattered the golden age of the antebellum rice kingdom, dealing the industry and its aristocracy a blow from which they never recovered. Unlike the Sea Islands, the mainland rice area was not occupied by federal forces until 1865. But army raids destroyed buildings, implements, and machinery, and the irrigation systems disintegrated on many plantations, leaving fields flooded and overgrown. The presence of federal troops on the islands provided a haven for escaping slaves, and some planters abandoned their estates altogether, either removing the slaves farther inland or leaving their lands in the hands of the blacks. Others, however, managed to continue rice planting until early 1865.

General William T. Sherman's army brought emancipation to the rice fields, and with it a rude awakening for the planters. More than in any other part of the South, the accumulated resentments of slavery burst forth in violence. In Georgetown,

plantation homes and meat houses were pillaged by the freedmen. Chicora Wood, the home plantation of Robert W. Allston
before his death in 1864, was ransacked by his slaves—every article of furniture was removed and his meticulous plantation
records destroyed. Allston's widow revealed some insight into
her slaves' behavior when she commented, "The conduct of the
negroes in robbing our house, store room, meat house, etc. and
refusing to restore anything shows you they *think it right* to
steal from us, to spoil us, as the Isrealites did the Egyptians." On
another Georgetown plantation, blacks "divided out the land
and . . . pulled down fences and would obey no driver."

Farther to the south, the magnificent plantation home at
Middleton Place near Charleston was burned to the ground and
the vaults in the family graveyard were broken open and the
bones scattered by the slaves, including some who had escaped
to enlist in the Union Army and who now returned with General Sherman to wreak vengeance. Williams Middleton suffered
the added indignity of being put on trial for his life by his slaves,
who debated the pros and cons of taking his life, weighing his
past kindnesses and severities, before finally allowing him to
depart.[6]

The same fate befell the extensive holdings of Charles Manigault. Even before the coming of federal troops, the overseers
had "lost all control" over "the turbulent Negroes." Manigault
had abandoned his plantations on the Cooper River and Argyle
Island to his slaves. Gathering his family in Charleston, he stood
helpless while his beautiful plantation homes were destroyed.
For Manigault, who viewed himself as the model of the paternalistic slaveowner, emancipation was indeed a moment of truth:

> For they broke into our well furnished residences on each
> plantation and stole or destroyed every thing therein. Nor,
> was there a solitary instance in either plantation of any one
> of our Negroes preserving for us a single thing whatever.
> . . . A Negro woman (Peggy) seized as her part of the spoils my
> wife's large and handsome mahogany bedstead and mattress
> and arranged it in her own Negro house on which she slept
> for some time. And in the pride of their freedom she got

some pink ribbons and tied in a dozen bows the wooly head of her daughter to the admiration of the other Negroes.

Manigault soon returned to Marshland, his farm on the Cooper River six miles above Charleston, but this caused only a temporary halt to the troubles:

> As soon as I retired, the Negroes rushed in, and continued their depredations until they had completely emptied the house for they had engaged a large boat, with some rogues and thieves from the city, and they carried off all the large furniture of every description, except Peggy's big bedstead, as she was not to be disturbed . . . during her slumbers, while in the enjoyment of her sweet dreams of freedom. . . . Frederick (the driver) was ringleader. . . . He encouraged all the Negroes to believe that the Farm, and every thing on it, now since Emancipation, belonged solely to them, and that their former owners had now no rights or control there whatever.

Other holdings of the Manigault family witnessed similar events. At Silk Hope, an unusual inland plantation growing rice and cotton forty miles from Charleston, whatever deference may have existed among the slaves vanished, as the bottom rail seemed to take a perverse pleasure in suddenly finding itself on top. Paintings, removed from the walls of the big house, were "hung up in their Negro houses, while some of the family portraits (as if to turn them into ridicule) they left out, night and day, exposed to the open air. Some of these paintings, they sold, to any one who would give a trifle for them, others they gave away, to any of the Negroes." At Gowrie and East Hermitage, Manigault's Savannah River plantations, it was Sherman's troops, rather than the slaves, who wreaked havoc, destroying the house, barn, and threshing mills, together with thousands of bushels of rice, while the blacks simply departed for Savannah and Hilton Head.[7]

At the close of the Civil War, the rice region was in turmoil, although, as a member of a Georgetown planter family noted, "no outrage has been committed against the whites except in the matter of property." Property, however, was the crux of the postemancipation conflict everywhere in the South. In the rice country it took on a distinctive cast. General Sherman's famous Field Order 15, of January, 1865, had set aside the Sea Islands and a portion of the coast for the exclusive settlement of blacks. Extending some thirty miles inland, the "Sherman reservation," with its promise of landownership for the emancipated slaves, encompassed virtually the entire rice region. During 1865 thousands of black families were settled on lands in the South Carolina and Georgia low country under the auspices of the Freedmen's Bureau and the army. Others simply seized plantations on the grounds that they had forty acres and a mule coming to them. "The negroes are carrying on things with a high hand," came a report from the Cooper River, "claiming everything as belonging to them, and feel no hesitation in ordering off the owners of the places, whenever they please." Allan C. Izard, a Savannah River rice planter, noted that the blacks were "incredulous as to *his* ownership of the land. . . . That feeling of security and independence," Izard concluded, "has to be eradicated. . . . The first thing to do is to get solid and safe possession of the land."[8]

Throughout the South, possession of the land was the focal point of conflict in early Reconstruction, but few regions witnessed as sustained a struggle as the South Carolina and Georgia low country. Here, where blacks had long enjoyed a unique degree of autonomy, black troops were spreading the gospel of land ownership. Federal authorities had sold land to Sea Island blacks during the war, and the Freedmen's Bureau seemed committed to further redistribution of the land. By the end of 1865, President Andrew Johnson, reversing the Bureau's initial policy, had pardoned the great majority of large planters and authorized the return of their lands. The actual process of restoration was a prolonged and bitter one, often requiring the intervention of Union soldiers. Throughout the low country, virtually the entire white population had fled, and blacks, who had cultivated the soil in 1865, had no intention of giving up their crops or abandoning their claim to the land. In Georgetown, when William Bull ordered recalcitrant freedmen off his plantation in January, 1866, they burned down his home. On the Santee River, when Captain

Thomas Pinckney returned to his plantation in 1866, blacks, who had sacked the big house the previous year, informed him that the land belonged to them, and that they would work for no white man. On the Sea Islands, freedmen barricaded themselves on plantations and drove off owners attempting to repossess them. At Delta plantation along the Savannah River, blacks in January, 1867, refused either to sign contracts for the coming year or to leave the premises. A reporter who witnessed the scene said the freedmen "swore . . . they would die where they stood before they would surrender their claims to the land." One declared, "we have but one master now—Jesus Christ—and he'll never come here to collect taxes or drive us off."[9]

Similar troubles developed on the rice plantations along the Combahee River, where, a Freedmen's Bureau officer reported in January, 1866, "there is a combination . . . to refuse work at any price." Not only were buildings burned on several Heyward family plantations, but blacks whom Charles Heyward had removed from the region at the outset of the Civil War "had promptly taken possession of the plantations" on their return early in 1866. Heyward's son Edward Barnwell Heyward decided to allow the freedmen to remain undisturbed, convinced that hunger would soon teach them that they could not subsist without white management. "I determined," he wrote, "that negroes like white people would only work from necessity." When he returned to the Combahee early in 1867, Heyward was "astonished to find the place in such excellent condition." Everything was in fine circumstances except, Heyward informed his wife, the blacks themselves:

It is very evident they are disappointed at my coming there. They were in hopes of getting off again this year and having the place to themselves. They are pretty well off, can easily make a living and go jobbing about. They received me very coldly, in fact it was some time before they came out of their houses to speak to me. . . . If I could meet with impudence, accompanied with intelligence, it wouldn't be so bad. But to find the brutish rice field negro familiar is perfectly disgusting. . . . As to work I do not imagine they will do much of it.

They can live so easily and upon so little that they are really independent.

The women, Heyward found, "wish to stay in the house or in the garden all the time," rather than laboring in the rice fields. And to make matters worse, one freedman informed Heyward "that the land ought to belong to the man who (alone) *could work it*. That I couldn't do more than sit in the house and tap my foot on the table and write on the paper etc." Because of the freedmen's spirit of defiance and the pending onset of Radical Reconstruction, crucial questions raised by emancipation—the right to the soil, the disposition of the crop, and labor's compensation—remained, Heyward recognized, unresolved. "You cannot be sure of any thing when negro rule commences," he wrote. "I still believe we can hold our own, *but* the negroes will have to enjoy more of *the fruits* than before." [10]

Eventually, many of the rice families regained possession of their lands, but output never reached its prewar levels. Numerous plantations remained uncultivated for years after the war, the land occupied by black squatters. Many who did try to resume planting were ruined by a crop failure in 1866, and an assault of caterpillars in 1869. Gloom settled over the old rice kingdom. "I can give you no adequate idea of the result of the emancipation, and the war generally upon us," wrote Robert Allston's son Benjamin. "From being one of the most wealthy Districts, I fear it will now rank as one of the most impoverished." To raise money, Benjamin's mother, Adele Allston, opened a girls' school in Charleston, but in 1869 the Allstons saw their vast holdings sold at auction, with only Chicora Wood remaining in the family. The Manigaults were likewise reduced to near poverty at the end of the Civil War. Charles and Louis Manigault attempted to make a living by selling consignments of Madeira wine to northern merchants. "I hear only of poverty and misery," Louis later wrote, "amongst those who were the richest and oldest families prior to the war." In 1869 South Carolina produced only thirty-two million pounds of rice—one quarter the total of ten years earlier—and Georgia's production had declined by more than half. [11]

The very collapse of rice production, however, pushed prices to unprecedented levels, and stimulated some planters to remain in business. Not surprisingly, the rice planters found "the labor question" a persistent source of trouble. With the end of the "game of confiscation," as one South Carolina planter called it, it was essential to reestablish labor discipline on the rice plantations: "Our place is to work; take hold and persevere; get labor of some kind; get possession of the places; stick to it; oust the negroes; and their ideas of proprietorship; . . . present a united and determined front; and make as much rice as we can. . . . Our plantations will have to be assimilated to the industrial establishment of other parts of the world, where the owner is protected by labour tallies, time tables, checks of all kinds and constant watchfulness."[12] But, however appealing in theory, such a mode of discipline ran headlong against the distinctive traditions of the low-country freedmen, and the labor shortage which appeared to grow worse as the years went on.

Low-country blacks found themselves with more alternative economic opportunities than most freedmen. To cultivate their lands, some planters simply rented the plantations to blacks for a share of the crop. At Gowrie plantation, which the Manigault family leased in 1867 to General George P. Harrison, five black foremen were placed in charge of operations, each hiring his own hands and directing labor as he saw fit, and the final crop was divided among the general, the foremen, and the laborers. On the Santee River one planter, because of the "disorganized condition of labor," simply turned his plantation over to freedmen to cultivate as they saw fit. Some planters, despairing of cultivating rice with free labor, sold their holdings to blacks. In Colleton County, by the early 1870s, several large plantations were operating under what a newspaper called "a sort of communism," with black laborers forming societies, electing officers, and purchasing the estates collectively. Other freedmen simply squatted on abandoned lands. In addition, the expansion of railroad building and phosphate mining in the region drew off many laborers, "and largely destroyed their value for systematic work," one planter complained.[13]

Many planters who did continue production discovered that

establishing a closely controlled wage system was simply out of the question. In the Sea Islands generally and on many rice plantations, a "two-day" system emerged, similar to labor-tenancy arrangements in other parts of the world. This made the laborer responsible for two days of work on the plantation in exchange for an allotment of land on which to grow his own crops. Additional plantation labor, if needed, was paid for in cash. For whites, the system at least secured a labor force which, being rooted in the soil, was available for harvest labor. One Edisto Island planter praised the system in 1872 for producing contented and efficient laborers: "I want no better laboring class than the one we now have, with their little farms around our broad acres; with their little comforts, their cow, pig and poultry. . . . The chief advantage . . . is the supply of *resident* labor, which is always at hand to be called into requisition."[14]

For blacks, the attraction of the two-day system lay in the autonomy it afforded when compared to wage or even share labor. As elsewhere in the South, autonomy was the lens through which rice workers viewed labor conditions during Reconstruction. Those who could rent or purchase land did so; those who could not sought modes of labor that secured the highest degree of personal independence. In the cotton districts, blacks rejected the customary organization of work—gang labor under the direction of an overseer—as incompatible with freedom. But in the low country, blacks desired labor to continue under the traditional task system that even under slavery had given them an exceptional degree of autonomy. On General John B. Gordon's Georgia rice plantation, "the negroes drove the overseer away, threatening his life, on account of some orders he had given about the particular way the rice was to be cultivated. They wanted to cultivate it in their own style." In the Georgetown region, a Freedmen's Bureau agent reported, the freedmen had "no just sense of the importance of persistent labor," preferring to regulate the pace of their work as they had done under slavery. "We want to work just as we have always worked," one declared.[15]

Like freedmen elsewhere, rice laborers assumed that emancipation would not mean a loss of privileges enjoyed under slavery. They insisted that they be allowed to retain access to lands for crops of their own, and rejected the authority of the owner or overseer to supervise their labor directly. "They absolutely deny my right to enforce any of my directions," complained a Georgia planter in 1866. In South Carolina, "they now positively refuse to make any contracts unless they have the control of the crops themselves; the planters to have little or nothing to say in the matter, but to receive a portion of the crop raised." There were also widespread complaints of low-country blacks thieving from the planters, a practice, it was charged, encouraged by crossroads country stores and trading vessels that anchored offshore to purchase stolen rice and meat. Efforts to impose plantation discipline were met with what planters called "insubordination." On one Georgetown plantation, reported an owner's agent, a woman "ordered me out of her task, saying if I come into her task again she would put me in the ditch, . . . a ploughman gets highly offended because I ask him if he has fed his oxen and does not answer the question at all, but asks me if I went in the field to see if they were fed." On a nearby plantation, the freedmen simply refused to listen to a reading of the contract by the owner, informing him "that they were free and would follow their own orders."[16]

The records of Weehaw plantation, near Georgetown, illustrate the intractable problems of labor control that persisted throughout Reconstruction. Owned by Henry A. Middleton, the plantation was abandoned at the close of the Civil War and cultivated in 1865 under the auspices of the Freedmen's Bureau, with the blacks receiving half the proceeds. Middleton was pardoned and restored to ownership at the end of the year, and for the next several seasons the plantation was managed by his cousin, Ralph Izard Middleton. As the latter's numerous reports make clear, one problem after another disrupted labor peace. First, there was politics. Even in 1866 the freedmen seemed aware of the implications of national debates over Reconstruction. "The negroes are very hard to manage," Middleton wrote on October 30, soon after northern congressional elections had resulted in a sweeping repudiation of Andrew Johnson's Reconstruction policies. "There is a good deal of fermentation still among them and radical success is at the bottom of it." Middleton was unable to call upon outside authorities to enforce his demands for plantation discipline. An army court did intervene to punish three women who assaulted him—they were sentenced to a month in prison. But when it came to organizing the day-to-day labor routine, he found himself powerless. As on other rice plantations, the freedmen insisted on determining the pace and pattern of work themselves, and resented any interference from the manager. As Middleton reported in November, 1866: "It is absolutely necessary to break up the old plantation gangs. As it now stands they cannot get over the notion that they are part proprietors. Finding fault with or punishing one excites the whole and the labor is entirely uncontrollable. . . . It appears that during the summer . . . they undertook, without saying one word to me, to divide them into eight gangs, and now they are outraged because I won't let them thresh and divide in the same way."[17]

Such problems convinced Middleton, like so many of his contemporaries, that a system of payment in monthly wages must be introduced, with half withheld until the crop had been marketed, so as to maintain labor discipline. "I do not see," he wrote, "how any difficulty could arise and you would have the whole crop management and disposal of it in your own hands." But the freedmen refused to agree to such a contract, and Middleton was forced to plant in 1867 on a crop-sharing basis, with blacks continuing to work in groups of their own choosing. By the end of 1867 Middleton was thoroughly disgusted with free labor: "They would never do more than half work. . . . The experience of every one about here is that this system won't work. The negroes can steal enough to live on but the proprietor will make nothing. [One gang stopped work recently] saying they were tired. What can one do in such a state of things. Their heads are full of politics and they have no idea of work until starvation forces them."

In 1868 Middleton was again forced to sign a contract on terms he considered disadvantageous, this time allowing each laborer to plant rice for himself, as well as performing tasks "as they were formerly required on the plantation." At the end of the year the crop was to be divided between proprietor and workers. Labor discipline continued to be a problem. In August the workers, fearing canal work would soon be asked of them, "managed so as to leave no time between hoeing and harvest." In 1869 Middleton once again found it impossible to move to a wage basis. "I think under the circumstances," he reported, "the condition of the country, the absence of law, the almost impossibility of getting full work from the negroes about here, the share system is the safest."[18]

The advent of Radical Reconstruction further complicated the labor situation. In Georgetown District, where nearly 3,000 blacks and only 457 whites were registered to vote in 1867, local offices quickly fell into black hands. "Two or three miserable Yankee negro politicians" took office in Georgetown, making the workers even more disorderly, according to Middleton. "They are constantly excited by the politicians for their own purposes. The negro magistrate or majesty as they call him tells them that no rice is to be shipped until it is all got out and divided 'according to law.'" The planter did not even enjoy control over the disposition of his own crop.[19]

Toward the end of 1869 Middleton hit upon another scheme for controlling black labor, this time combining a wage system with a plantation store: "This contract system will have to be abandoned and a store run with wages tho nominally high yet practically brought down to a moderate rate by the percentage on the goods furnished." So in January, 1870, he drafted a new labor agreement, under which the laborers would receive tickets worth fifty cents, redeemable at the plantation store, for each day worked. Each hand would also be allowed to grow one acre of rice and one of corn. There would, however, be no official written contract, "so that whenever a negro misbehaves he may be dismissed." Here was the system of labor discipline for which Middleton had yearned. There was just one problem: the freedmen absolutely refused to sign, and every day's delay threatened the next year's crop. Finally Middleton, once again, had to surrender: "The negroes object so strongly to wages, it is so late and the labor is so demoralized that I think almost any sort of contract is better than the risk of losing more time and perhaps the labor entirely and coming out minus. I will therefore have, I suppose, to submit to last year's contract with this improvement if I can enforce it, that no hand contracting is to do *any job* off of the plantation."[20]

Solidarity, an ability to use the requirements of the planting season to their own advantage, control of local government, and the opening up of economic alternatives in the neighborhood had all strengthened the freedmen's hand. At least Middleton had no illusions about the nature of their relationship. "The fact is," he wrote his cousin, "this is a continuous struggle where the planter is all the time at a great disadvantage." One sign of this disadvantage was that "many planters" were "renting their lands to the negroes and one or two plantations bought by the land commission attract their labor." As a result, the labor shortage grew increasingly severe. One planter was reduced to "trying to induce, with extra pay, whisky, etc., negroes to work for him." At the end of 1871 Middleton lamented, "The negroes do pretty much as they please and laugh at threats of dismissal as there are any number of places where they can go."[21]

Eventually, by establishing a plantation store, Middleton did manage to entice many of his workers into debt, resulting, he reported, in their being "very much improved in *temper*" and more obedient to his orders. But he never did place Weehaw plantation on a cash wage basis. "The negroes," he reported at the end of 1874, "know that wages mean work or no pay and are averse to them."[22]

Along the Combahee and Ashepoo rivers during the early 1870s, however, a number of planters did succeed in retaining control of thousands of acres of land and employing hundreds of wage laborers, who lived scattered across the estates in little villages. The Combahee presented a complex pattern of labor relations that defies generalization. Alongside the wage labor plantations—still operating on the task system—there were estates conducted on the two-day basis, blacks owning their own farms purchased from the state land commission, and many living on small plots in nearby pinelands and engaging in occasional plantation labor.[23]

The Combahee was the scene of labor troubles throughout Reconstruction. Blacks, as we have seen, staked a claim to Edward B. Heyward's plantation in 1867. Two of James B. Heyward's overseers were murdered on a nearby estate. Black laborers on the Ashepoo hauled W. J. Whipper, a prominent black politician, into court in 1872, charging him with refusing to compensate them for their labor. And in 1873, when the northern reporter Edward King visited the extensive holdings of J. B. Bissell, comprising thirty-five hundred acres and employing eight hundred hands at harvest time, he found the workers keeping up "an incessant jargon with one another" in the fields, indulging in "a running fire against the field-master." Throughout the region, he reported, planters "found great difficulty in keeping the labor organized and available." By 1876, however, the labor situation had shifted somewhat in the planters' favor. By recruiting workers from outside the region, they had managed to counteract the labor shortage. The depression that began in 1873, moreover, reduced the region and many freedmen to poverty. One report from the Combahee in March, 1876, spoke of "the lamentable condition of hundreds if not thousands both white and colored now without bread to eat or provisions to make a crop on and no money to buy with and at a loss to know what to do."[24]

For several years planters in the region had adopted the practice of paying their workers in checks, which could either be redeemed at plantation stores or exchanged for cash some years in the future. The check system had been outlawed by the Reconstruction South Carolina legislature and was considered pernicious by many forward-looking planters. "When the laborer gets his money," a Sea Island planter advised in 1872, "let him go ... where he likes—never check upon your own store; he has worked cheap enough; do not apply the extortioner's scissors to his earnings." It was the practice of payment in checks, coupled with a wage reduction from fifty to forty cents for day laborers, which triggered the Combahee strikes of 1876.[25]

In May, 1876, in the midst of the hoeing season, and at a time when unusually high tides had flooded some fields and necessitated emergency repairs in the dikes along the Combahee, the day laborers on New Port plantation came out on strike, demanding payment in cash and an increase in wages. Owned by Edward B. Heyward until his death in 1871, the plantation was now managed by his brother-in-law Allan C. Izard, and the strikers held their first meeting at Izard's plantation store. Here they elected officers, drafted a letter to Governor Daniel H. Chamberlain, and signed an "original agreement": "We the undersigned do hereby strike from this day forward, and until we receive full wages for a day's services, and we further agree not to return to work until the planters agree to pay us for hoeing the rice from 50 cts to 75 cts per half acre, according to the quality and condition of the land. We numbers but three hundred laborers with daily accessions. Our reasons for striking is our employers reduced our wages to 40 cts per day, a figure at which we cannot live." It was rumored that the statement had been drafted by Alexander P. Holmes, a black teacher on the New Port plantation who had represented Colleton County in the legislature from 1870 to 1874.[26]

The strike, according to a reporter for the Charleston *News and Courier*, originated among the day laborers, "a class of negroes who live in the pine lands and do their own cropping and in the working season eke out their subsistence by hiring by the day to the planter." The day laborers had been the target of the wage reduction; regular hands with yearly contracts had not been affected. But as the strike spread to nearby plantations on the Combahee, then to the Ashepoo River and finally into Beaufort County, numerous contract hands joined in. In the days that followed, hundreds of blacks marched through the rice district with horns and drums, some armed with clubs, urging plantation workers to leave the fields. On some plantations, the response was overwhelming. One planter reported that fifty-three blacks came to his place and "had quite a parade. After speaking and the like, every one of the men there joined them."[27]

As they marched, the strikers sang a song reportedly originating among Mississippi Democrats in the bloody Redemption campaign of 1875:

> A charge to keep I have,
> A negro to maintain
> A never-dying thirst for power
> To bind him with a chain.

To serve the present age
Our pockets we must fill
We'll make them work for wages now,
And never pay the bill

Arm me with jealous care
To make him know his place;
And of thy servant, Lord, prepare
To rule the negro race.

Help us to rob and cheat
The nigger on the sly
Assured if they don't vote for us
They shall forever die.

With its evocation of the overthrow of Reconstruction in Mississippi, and the design among whites to "rule the negro race," the song created immense "excitement" when sung by the strikers. "One colored man," a journalist reported, "said he didn't know what the trouble was about until he heard the song."[28]

Not all rice workers, however, were swept into the strike. On some plantations a number of laborers under yearly contracts remained in the fields. Unlike the day laborers, whose small plots of land off the plantations gave them a degree of economic autonomy, the yearly workers could not afford to risk eviction from the plantation in a period of economic depression. One such laborer wrote Governor Chamberlain that J. B. Bissell, for whom he had worked for several years, had "bin a grate help to our poor collord people" by advancing supplies and credit. But a crowd of five hundred strikers had halted work on the Bissell plantation, "and we can't get nothing. . . . We are a poor people have home nor contry nor money eder. Do tell me how we ar to do for a lively hood." On some plantations, blacks who continued to work were dragged from the fields and beaten by the strikers; on others, they were forced to join the marchers and warned not to return to work. In most cases, only working day laborers were assaulted, while contract hands were not interfered with. And on the plantations where wages had not been reduced, labor continued uninterrupted. No violence was threatened to any white person, indeed the strikers were said to be "perfectly civil and polite" to the planters.[29]

The work stoppage and beatings placed Governor Chamberlain in a delicate position. On the one hand, local planters and several black victims demanded armed protection for laborers willing to work. On the other, the large majority of the rice workers appear to have supported the strikers, and with a difficult reelection campaign in the offing, their sentiments could hardly be ignored. From the outset of the strike, according to one report, "politics was largely mixed with their harangues and proceedings." Among local political leaders, only Beaufort legislator Thomas Hamilton, himself a black rice planter, opposed the strike. At one gathering, Hamilton delivered what a white observer termed a "wise, manly and courageous" speech, warning the strikers not to pay heed to "hellish politicians" and exhorting them to return to work. But former legislator Alexander P. Holmes had played a part in the strike's beginning, and another "influential colored man," Edward Bowers, told a strike meeting that forty cents was an inadequate daily wage. Thomas Richardson, a black carpenter who represented Colleton in the legislature, urged the freedmen to remain on strike, and the white trial justice, L. Shuman, pledged that as long as he remained in office, "he would not do anything to have them arrested, and he hoped they would hold out." Some, indeed, blamed the whole affair on the prolabor Shuman, recently dismissed by Chamberlain in an effort to placate local planter opinion, but who, for the moment, retained his office.

Chamberlain at this point was engaged in a complicated political balancing act, seeking Democratic endorsement for reelection, yet knowing that he would need the black vote as well. He instructed Sheriff J. K. Terry to inform the laborers that he recognized their right to strike, but not "to make others join them against their will." Amnesty was promised for offenses already committed, but those who continued to violate the law would be arrested. At the same time, Chamberlain, through the sheriff, conveyed to the strikers his sympathy "with all who are struggling for a bare subsistence."[30]

By refusing to send troops as planters demanded, Chamberlain retained the affection of the strikers. Two black leaders of the anti-Chamberlain faction in Colleton's Republican party, William A. Driffle, a prosperous mulatto carpenter who had served in the state legislature, and Nathaniel B. Myers, another "well-to-do freeborn mulatto," were shouted down at one meeting and "run off of Combahee" by the strikers. Possibly their wealth and color had something to do with their reception, but a report to the Governor stressed the political dimension: "The people . . . all say that any one that is against Governor Chamberlain is against us." For their part, the planters bitterly resented Chamberlain's failure to enforce the law. Unable to obtain protection for those willing to work, most planters acceded to the strikers' demands.[31]

By the end of May, work had resumed at the traditional rate of fifty cents per day, although on some plantations the check system was still in force. No one was prosecuted for acts of violence and soon afterwards, Alexander P. Holmes, whom many planters accused of instigating the entire affair, was appointed a local trial justice by the governor. Chamberlain's lenient course alienated the rice plantation owners and played some part in the eventual decision of the Democratic party not to "fuse" with reform-minded Republicans. (Local storekeepers, who resented the planters' attempt, through the check system, to monopolize the trade of the freedmen, seem to have supported the governor's stance.) As one planter complained, the whole affair demonstrated that under Republican rule, planters simply could not count for protection upon state or local authorities: "Our large and valued interests, to ourselves, to the state, and the colored people themselves, are at the mercy of any ignorant mob that chooses to raid over us. And the power in that county that ought to be exercised in behalf of peace and good government, is wrapt up in the selfish consideration of their own interests in the coming election."[32]

By late August, 1876, when labor trouble again broke out on the Combahee, the political climate in South Carolina had been transformed. Whites favoring a "straight-out" campaign for white supremacy modeled on the Mississippi election of 1875, had gained the upper hand in the Democratic party. In August, General Wade Hampton was nominated to run for governor, and armed rifle clubs began demanding "division of time" at Republican meetings.[33] The atmosphere of political tension and interracial violence, the heightened anxiety of blacks and whites alike about the future of the state, made the next wave of strikes appear even more threatening than the troubles of May.

The second round of strikes in the rice fields began on August 18, only two days after Hampton's nomination, but the immediate cause was more economic than political. The harvest of rice had begun, and "the planters' need of help had become imperative." Blacks on the extensive holdings of J. B. Bissell, where labor checks redeemable at his store or in cash in 1880 were still in use, demanded that the wage for harvest labor be raised from one dollar to one dollar fifty cents a task, payable in cash. To the planters, this seemed "an exorbitant price for a task that an ordinary field hand can easily accomplish before noon." But virtually all Bissell's workers walked out of the fields. Then on Sunday, August 20, at a plantation in nearby Green Pond, those remaining at work were attacked by strikers armed with clubs and whips. The laborers, moreover, refused to allow rice already gathered to be forwarded to market. Then the strike spread to Clay Hall plantation, owned by local trial justice Henry H. Fuller. Fuller's plantation operated on the two-day system, but his workers now demanded additional pay for harvest labor. This, Fuller's plantation manager believed, was "an atrocious demand as they are in full and quiet possession of the land and houses." On Fuller's estate, the strikers demanded two dollars a task and drove from the fields those who wished to continue working.[34]

Since, as one newspaper reported, "the negro militia of the district is composed in great part of the strikers," the planters could expect little assistance from the forces of law and order. Instead, trial justice Fuller, acting with Beaufort deputy sheriff B. B. Sams, decided to call out the Democratic Green Pond Rifle Club to restore order. If the intention was to cow the strikers into submission, the miscalculation could not have been more complete. Proceeding to Fuller's plantation at Sheldon, Fuller and Sams arrested five ringleaders. But a crowd of blacks soon appeared, released the prisoners, and drove trial justice, sheriff, constables, and rifle club to seek refuge in the plantation thresh- ing mill. Fortunately for the imprisoned whites, Congressman Robert Smalls, the most prominent low-country black political leader during Reconstruction, and black Lieutenant Governor Robert Gleaves, were at that moment attending a political rally at nearby Walterboro. Smalls, who also served as a major general in the militia, was ordered by state Attorney General William Stone to call out troops. Instead, he proceeded to Sheldon, where he found three hundred blacks threatening to tear down the fences and attack the forty or so whites armed with rifles, six- shooters, and shotguns. "The presence of these armed whites," Smalls later reported, "did much to alarm and excite the strik- ers." One told him, "These rebels here are trying to drive us into the field."[35]

Smalls and Gleaves eventually interposed themselves be- tween the two groups to prevent violence. Although some in the crowd "did not want to respect him," Smalls convinced the strikers to allow the rifle company to depart and the ten ring- leaders for whom warrants had been issued to surrender them- selves to the sheriff. But his report to Governor Chamberlain on the whole affair made clear where his sympathies lay. Smalls pronounced trial justice Fuller incapable of dispensing impartial justice and demanded his removal: "He is a large planter and one who issues checks to his laborers; therefore there must be, natu- rally, dissatisfaction on the part of laborers brought before him." He excoriated the planters for issuing checks and then charging "exorbitant prices" in their plantation stores. Bacon, generally selling for ten cents per pound, was twenty-five cents at Bissell's store, and molasses, regularly forty cents per gallon, was three times that price, "and other articles in proportion." The aim of the check system, Smalls believed, was to make it "impossible for the laborers to obtain any of the necessaries of life except through the planters."[36]

Thanks to Smalls's intervention, the threat of violence passed, the planters agreed to pay their workers in cash, and the strike appeared, for the moment, to be over. But the disposition of the cases of the ten arrested leaders hardly inspired confidence among the planters. Promised by Smalls that he would personally meet whatever bail was set, the ten were marched the fifteen miles to Beaufort, Smalls's political stronghold, where mayor, police force, and magistrates were all black. If a focal point of black power existed during Reconstruction, it lay in Beaufort, the heart of low-country black life, whose streets were lined by the graceful town houses of the rice aristocracy. "Here the revolution penetrated to the quick," commented newspaperman Edward King in 1873. "One of the most remarkable revolutions ever recorded in history has occurred. A wealthy and highly prosperous community has been reduced to beggary; its vassals have become its lords." Throughout these years, Beaufort was a byword for black self-assurance and pride. Blacks on his Combahee plantation, Edward B. Heyward had commented some years earlier, had acquired the " 'Beaufort manner'. . . . They are constantly in Beaufort and quite so much the worse for their good."

On the evening of August 23, the ten arrested men arrived in Beaufort, to be arraigned before a black trial justice. But, as rice planter William Elliott recounted, "they were certainly never placed in jail, and I am informed that the crowd on the streets openly sympathized with and applauded them, and publicly announced that they should not go to trial." Moreover, those workers who had been beaten in the fields and subsequently lodged complaints were suddenly found to be extremely reluctant to press charges. The next morning, before the sheriff had even arrived at court, the black trial justice dismissed all charges and the prisoners went free. "No examination, no trial, no punishment —nothing but a gross outrage upon law in the name of law, and a sweeping invitation to all others to commit like acts of violence," was William Elliott's comment.[37]

Once again, political realities had prevented planters from calling on the state to force their laborers back to work. Chamberlain, it is true, had appointed men like Fuller to local office as part of his attempt to woo conservative support. But the militia, local black leaders, and judicial authorities sympathized with the strikers. Troops could not be sent in to discipline them, convictions of the leaders could not be obtained, and, on their return to the Combahee, the ringleaders resumed "chairing large meetings" of the laborers, as one disgusted planter reported.

Even trial justice Fuller found it impossible to compel his laborers to resume work. The workers simply told his agent, B. F. Sellers, that "Robert Smalls tells them not to do so," and Fuller had to admit that "if the hands are arrested and sent to Beaufort . . . they will at once be released and sent back perhaps to do worse."

Smalls, in fact, had attended a meeting of a "labor society" on the Beaufort side of the Combahee River, and told the strikers, in good free labor language, that while they had a perfect right to organize and quit work, "if anybody chose to work for ten cents a day they had no right to take the law into their own hands . . . other men were as free as they were." But Sellers was right to perceive a relationship between Smalls's political authority and the strikers' own ability to do as they pleased. Smalls was a living symbol of black power, of the revolution that had put the bottom rail on top, at least in local politics. The only remedy for the rice planters, Sellers believed, was state or federal intervention, "so that the people (who are very ignorant) will see that Robert Smalls etc. are not the law nor have they the power to administer it."[38]

For several days, labor trouble subsided on the Combahee, but the outbreak there had an infectious impact on other parts of the low country. On a Cooper River rice plantation near Charleston the workers, led by local political figure George Sass, demanded an increase in harvest pay, and prevented those willing to work at the old price from going to the fields. Then trouble erupted once again on the Combahee. Beginning on August 28, the cycle of strikes, marches, and the beating of workers who remained in the fields resumed. Planters feared it would spread to the entire rice district of South Carolina and Georgia. The strikers now made no distinction between those few plantations where checks were still in use, and the larger number where payment was weekly and in cash. With the harvest at a standstill, the planters' plight was becoming desperate. They still refused to raise wages to one dollar fifty per task, a price which, one group of planters claimed, would "ruin the rice interest already jeopardized by many unfortunate events."[39]

Trouble persisted well into the month of September. The

black militia continued to be of no use at all to the planters, since, as one complained, militia officers were "actively engaged with the rioters." When Governor Chamberlain called upon Charleston's chief constable James Low to take a posse and arrest perpetrators of violence, Low wisely demurred. Such a course might spark off all-out racial warfare: "Should we fail . . . we had conjured a Frankenstein who would not down at our bidding." Ironically the rice planters, who had long demanded "home rule" for their state, now called for the dispatch of federal troops as the only way to maintain the peace.[40]

On September 7 occurred a virtual repetition of the dangerous events at Fuller's plantation in August. Once again, a deputy sheriff, this time A. C. Schaffer, sought, with a posse, to arrest a number of strikers. Once again a crowd of blacks imprisoned them on a plantation, this time one belonging to J. B. Bissell. Once again an armed rifle club was on the scene. And, as in August, it took the intervention of Robert Smalls to release the prisoners and prevent bloodshed. A planter who was there described the scene:

> We were literally beseiged, not a man being allowed to go out of the enclosure. A howling, raving, infuriated crowd of demons rushing up to the fence, using every imaginable curse and imprecation against the whites personally and collectively, coupled with the most repulsive obscenity. When night arrived the scene beggars description, the crowd having grown bolder, kept up a continuous howl cursing individually every man whom they knew. . . . Such is the state of feeling and you will see that it may at any moment precipitate the people of this section into a war of the races.

As in August, Smalls convinced the crowd to disperse, the armed whites were permitted, two by two, to leave for their homes, and five men accused of assault were arrested. But at Walterboro, trial justice Alexander P. Holmes, the black teacher and former legislator who had assisted the strikers in May, dropped all charges, so "the rioters went home to commence anew." Meanwhile, some Combahee plantations did resume work at the rate, considered ruinous by planters, of one dollar fifty per day.[41]

Throughout September, deputy sheriff Schaffer reported, the rice region remained in "a state of uneasiness and ferment," with "no good feeling" between planter and laborer. Schaffer, editor of the Walterboro *News* and a political ally of Governor Chamberlain, blamed the white rifle clubs for much of the trouble. Their appearance had convinced blacks that whites intended to compel them to labor at whatever rate "the planters see fit to offer." Against such threats, strikers retaliated with talk of burning the threshing mills and barns. One local black leader, former trial justice Adams Smith, was said to have remarked that if one striker were killed, "not a white man would be left" in the rice region. Attorney General Stone was greatly perplexed. "I confess I do not know what it is best to do," he wrote Chamberlain in mid-September. A force could be gathered from the white rifle clubs that, by "killing some of the rioters," might "put them down for a while." But, Stone concluded, in a masterpiece of understatement, this might be "a desperate and perhaps dangerous gamble."

The labor turmoil, indeed, presented Governor Chamberlain with a series of insoluble dilemmas. On the one hand, an outbreak of real violence would further discredit his beleaguered regime in the eyes of the nation. As Charleston constable Low warned him, "the planters would be ruined, the factors and bankers in Charleston would suffer enormous losses, and the capitalists of New York who have made the advances would join with them in one general outcry against the state administration." Rice was simply too important to be left at the mercy of the rice workers. On the other hand, facing a difficult reelection campaign, Chamberlain needed every Republican vote he could muster, and in South Carolina, Republican votes meant black votes. For their part, Democrats seized upon Chamberlain's inaction as a club with which to batter the state government. Nothing was being done to protect the rights of property and preserve order, said the Charleston *News and Courier*, because "the rioters are voters, the election approaches, the Republican officials are determined not to alienate from themselves their most efficient supporters." The implication was clear: only a change of administration could bring peace to the rice region.[42]

In the whole Combahee affair, as a South Carolina journalist later recalled, "politics and labor demands oddly mixed." Indeed, it appears there was some connection between those who remained at work, and those blacks who favored Hampton for governor. On the Fuller plantation, the black foreman, Peter Jones, who for two years had been paying workers in checks, also delivered Democratic campaign speeches in 1876. When Bissell sought to break the strike on his plantation, he sent for members of a black Democratic club in Walterboro and called on the white Democratic rifle club to protect them. But, as he later recounted, "they were not allowed to work by the Republican negroes. . . . Those who were democrats were not allowed to work for me because they were democrats, and they were working for a democrat." Toby Coker, a black Democratic strikebreaker who had been whipped on the Bissell place, reported that during the beating the strikers harangued him about politics. Although they were "low country colored people, and I couldn't understand them well" Coker believed "they said that no damn democrats should come down there to work." To the strikers, Coker was a strikebreaker, a Democrat, and a cultural outsider—three times an alien in the tightly knit community of the low-country freedmen.[43]

Earlier in Reconstruction, a northern planter had witnessed a number of strikes among plantation workers and observed that to the blacks, no sin was more deprecated than "going back on their color." Chandra Jayawardena, in his studies of Indian plantation laborers in British Guiana, concludes that the plantation itself has a strong tendency to generate ideologies of equality and a strong sense of group solidarity among its labor force. The very conditions of their lives, their "social equivalence" on the plantation, generates an intense sense of cohesiveness, and their unequal power in relation to the planter class forces the laborers to fall back upon collective unity as their only available weapon. In the rice kingdom, the sense of solidarity was intensified by the distinctiveness of the low country's black community. This collective sense helps explain why the great majority of the rice workers supported the strikes, and the strikers felt themselves justified in coercing those who remained at work. The strikers, according to one report, believed "that they have perfect 'right to do anything they choose with their own color,' and become beside themselves with fury at the sight of a white man undertaking to interfere." Indeed, nonstriking workers themselves did not appear to desire white intervention, even when the alternative was a beating.[44]

The same sense of solidarity generated intense antagonism toward blacks who supported the Democratic party. Despite Hampton's eloquent appeals for racial harmony and his pledges to respect the constitutional rights of black citizens, very few freedmen appear to have supported him in 1876. Those who did met with unbridled hostility. As one Democratic observer put it, the black community "treated them as deserters of their race and of their party, and of their political friends. . . . Those who showed any disposition at all to come over to the democratic side were denounced as traitors." Even prominent blacks were shouted down in the low country when they sought to speak for Hampton. When Martin Delany, in October, appeared on Edisto Island to support the Democrats, "the drums of the militia were beaten and he was 'howled down.'" In the Combahee region, Hampton himself received a hostile reception. In September, the Democratic candidate had launched his triumphant swing through the state, accompanied by rifle clubs and mass processions. In October, Hampton invaded the low country. On his first foray into the Combahee region, with some six hundred cavalry, he was heckled and forced to retire. Hampton later returned with over three thousand armed men, and gave his speech without interruption. When he reached Beaufort at the end of the month, Hampton was "surrounded by black people with black looks, made to feel hatred every minute and at every step." Unlike the plantation laborers in Jayawardena's British Guiana, South Carolina blacks enjoyed political power and were not anxious to see it stripped away.[45]

Republican political power, after all, had helped create the context within which successful collective action was possible. Nowhere was the difference made by Reconstruction more evident than in the rice kingdom itself during 1876. The rice region, of course, transcended state boundaries. Its heart stretched along the low country on both sides of the Georgia-South Carolina border, and many planter families owned properties in both states. But in 1876 there was a fundamental difference: South Carolina was still under Republican control, while Georgia had been "redeemed." A look at the situation at Gowrie plantation, just on the Georgia side of the border, illustrates the crucial importance of this fact.

Beginning in 1869 Charles Manigault, Gowrie's owner, had rented the plantation to Daniel Heyward. The elder Manigault died in 1874, and his son Louis decided to operate it himself, along with James B. Heyward. On arriving at Gowrie in January, 1876, Manigault found the lessee had let the place fall into ruin. Nor had Heyward, apparently, been an effective disciplinarian, for one of the first things Manigault did was "free the place from boisterous and turbulent negroes" who had settled there. The black tenants had spent more time on their own crops than in working the rice fields, marketing their produce in Savannah by way of a "regular trading boat" operated by the husband of one of the former slaves. Manigault was able to induce the resident blacks to return to field labor. To repair the dikes and canals— labor blacks objected to performing—he hired several squads of Irish laborers. These he found far superior to the blacks in productivity and demeanor: "There is no talking, as with negroes, no trifling, but the work goes on rapidly and in a serious manner." By July James B. Heyward, managing Gowrie for Manigault, could report, "We have the labor under full control, and this is a very important item."[46]

The outbreak of labor strife on the Combahee in August posed a serious threat to tranquility in the Georgia rice region. But Georgia was not South Carolina. The Redeemers there, having taken power in 1872, had effectively restricted black political participation, slashed the tax rate, and gutted social services. One institution did, however, escape the parsimonious hand of Redemption: the military. Under Governor James M. Smith, tens of thousands of dollars were appropriated to purchase rifles, pistols, and ammunition for the state militia. Perhaps not coincidentally, the bulk of letters received by Governor Smith in August, and September, 1876, during the Combahee strikes, concerned requests for arms and ammunition from militia companies throughout the state. As the captain of one company explained, "The organization exerts a good influence upon the morals and deportment of our new citizens."[47]

While the South Carolina rice district was in turmoil, quiet reigned in Georgia. Louis Manigault, Gowrie's owner, explained why: "We were exempt from all disturbances of this kind. A little disaffection evinced itself on the Cheves plantation low down the Savannah River, but it was nipped in the bud by the negroes being made to understand that a company of soldiers was ready at a moment's notice in Savannah, to cross the river, and sweep out of the plantation all disaffected negroes, not only there, but if necessary troops would scour the entire Savannah Swamp. This was strictly true, and had the desired effect." While Combahee planters were paying one dollar fifty or two dollars per task to get their rice harvested, the cost of day labor at Gowrie remained at seventy cents for most of the summer, and never exceeded ninety at the height of the harvest season. Gowrie's crop in 1876 was not a particularly lucrative one, for a storm in June had flooded the fields. Manigault was unable to repay all the money he had borrowed from a Charleston merchant at the beginning of the year. But on the Combahee, J. B. Bissell lost nearly fifty thousand dollars in 1876, and nearly all the planters, according to one report, did not recoup their expenses. Had Manigault's workers had the opportunity to strike, the situation might have been even bleaker at Gowrie. As he noted, "Had we been compelled to pay during our harvest the Combahee prices for labor it would have cost us upwards of $2000 more for labor upon our plantation books."[48]

South Carolina planters, of course, were hardly unaware of the contrast between their plight in 1876 and what had happened in Georgia. In the winter of 1876–1877, as the fate of government in both South Carolina and Washington hung in the balance, the rice planters looked forward to easier times if Wade Hampton acceded to office. The Charleston *News and Courier* insisted that Hampton would provide the military protection

Chamberlain had failed to supply: "Throughout the strike the impotence of the State government was miserably evident. . . . Chamberlain's rule . . . would leave the Combahee section exposed to the strikes and riots which injured the planters last year. The simple recognition of Hampton as Governor . . . would give factors and planters such confidence that planting would go on more vigorously than before strikes were thought of." Interestingly, rice planter Thomas Hamilton, the only black politician of note actually to oppose the strikers in 1876, played a part in Hampton's eventual victory, deserting the Republican legislature during the winter for the rival Democratic House, helping give the latter body a quorum and the appearance of bipartisan respectability.[49]

With the advent of Hampton and the collapse of the state Republican party, scenes such as those witnessed on the Combahee in 1876 could never be repeated. Blacks in Georgetown, Colleton, and Beaufort counties did continue to serve in local office, the legislature, and even Congress for another two decades. But with state government firmly in the hands of the Redeemers, there was no question where its sympathies would lie in subsequent labor disputes. Although urban workers were, on occasion, able to organize effectively after the overthrow of Reconstruction, the possibility of collective action by rural laborers was all but eliminated. When strikes were attempted, they were suppressed with ruthless brutality. In South Carolina, local sheriffs and the state militia were employed time and again to crush efforts in the 1880s and 1890s to organize black agricultural workers. A strike for higher wages among Louisiana sugar workers in 1887 led to a massacre in which over one hundred blacks were gunned down by the militia and white vigilantes. Four years later, fifteen leaders of an Arkansas cotton pickers' strike were killed, including nine who were lynched after being arrested by the local sheriff.[50]

To white southerners, and black leaders like Booker T. Washington, it became axiomatic after Redemption that black workers, unlike whites, "never strike." As the South Carolina agricultural reformer and political leader D. Wyatt Aiken put it in 1883, northern workers were joining unions in unprecedented numbers, making them "tenfold more exacting than at the South. . . . Southern farmers are generally lucky on that score."[51] But more than luck was involved. The history of labor conflict after Reconstruction offers an object lesson in the ways the state can be employed to render labor militancy virtually impossible.

Yet the ultimate fate of the rice kingdom also underscores the limits of even brutally repressive force, for control of government was not enough to save the low-country rice planters in the long run. Thanks in part to a tariff on imported rice, production did recover somewhat by the end of the 1870s, although it remained far below the levels of the antebellum years. But the rehabilitation of the rice kingdom would have required a vast expenditure of capital, which neither the state or federal governments, nor private interests, were willing to undertake, especially since virgin lands in Louisiana, Texas, and Arkansas were now being opened to rice cultivation. Louisiana's planters, financed by investment from London, employed advanced machinery, which dramatically increased the yield per laborer. The state's rice output tripled during the 1880s, while that of South Carolina and Georgia stagnated. By 1890, the old rice kingdom produced only one-third of the nation's crop. Then in the 1890s and early twentieth century, a series of devastating hurricanes destroyed the dikes and floodgates, delivering the coup de grace to the surviving low-country rice plantations. The last remaining rice planter, Theodore D. Ravenal, ceased operations in 1927.[52]

Years before, however, twilight had descended upon the rice kingdom. During Reconstruction, increasing numbers of blacks had been able to rent or purchase small plots of land, and the Redeemers were not able to reverse the process. It was one thing for the state to suppress labor organization, but quite another to intervene directly to dispossess black renters and owners, or impose day-to-day discipline on the rice plantations, especially with competition from Louisiana rising, capital investment unavailable, and blacks retaining, for a generation, a considerable degree of local political power. Despite his enthusiasm for Governor Hampton, Ralph I. Middleton was forced to conclude that the Redeemer governor "can't do much for our *pockets*. . . . I don't believe that rice can be cultivated profitably for many years longer without compulsory labor, which we don't seem at all likely to have."

Not that the Hampton regime failed to take steps to prevent a repetition of the events of 1876. As Robert Smalls told the visiting member of the British Parliament, Sir George Campbell, in 1878, the black militia companies had been disarmed by the state government, leaving the volunteer rifle clubs—really white Democratic political associations—with a monopoly of armed force in the low country. One rice planter told Campbell that Redemption had made a difference. In 1876, "his manager could get no assistance from the Radical Government; so he was obliged to yield for that time, but he has since come back to the old rates, and all has gone smoothly; there has been no more trouble." Yet there were limits to what even Redemption could accomplish in post-Civil War America. In the end, the great plantations fell to pieces, their lands rented or sold to blacks. Here in the low country, a unique combination of circumstances—initial federal policy, the collapse of rice production, a prolonged period of local black political power, and the cohesion and militancy of the black community—promoted black land-ownership. As a result, the adjustment to abolition took a distinctive form and, more than in any other region of the South, the freedmen succeeded in shaping social life and labor relations in accordance with their own traditions and aspirations.[53]

By 1890, 72 percent of the farms in Beaufort County, 71 percent in Colleton, and 81 percent in Bryan County, Georgia, were cultivated by their owners, the vast majority of them blacks. The low-country peasantry lived on an essentially subsistence basis, raising their own vegetables and poultry, while at the same time cultivating some cotton or rice and engaging in occasional wage labor on surviving plantations or in Charleston and Savannah, to raise necessary cash. Because wildlife was so abundant in the endless pine forests and streams of the low country, they could supplement their diet by hunting and fishing. Access to land and alternative means of subsistence made the low-country peasantry independent of the oppressive crop lien system and impervious to demands for steady wage labor. "The

Negroes there," a Georgia planter observed, "will not work for wages, as they can live almost without work on fish, crawfish and oysters; a little patch of cotton furnishing them the means for tobacco and clothing." The result of all this, one newspaper complained, was that low-country blacks had become "perfectly independent of the white man."[54]

Although it might seem foolhardy to introduce the term "peasantry" into the analysis of the postemancipation South (since students of peasants have a difficult time defining precisely what the word means), there are obvious parallels between the political economy of the low-country blacks, the Caribbean's "reconstituted peasantry," and small-scale family farming partially independent of the marketplace in other historical contexts.[55] Low-country blacks suffered from the same debilitating disadvantages that afflict peasant agriculture throughout the world, among them a credit system that made direct access to capital impossible, an inability to invest in fertilizer or machinery, vulnerability to the vagaries of the national and international markets, and the demands for taxation of an oppressive state. Blacks in the low country, it is true, were able to exercise more local political authority than many peasantries in the generation following Reconstruction, but on the state and federal levels they were powerless. They were unable to use the state to bolster their own form of production as, for example, the Populists later sought to do, and as Danish and Eastern European peasant parties accomplished with some success in this century, providing beleaguered peasants with state financing for credit, marketing, and land acquisition.[56]

Such effective use of political power was completely out of the question for the low-country freedmen after the end of Reconstruction. Like its Caribbean counterpart, the peasantry survived, but its growth was stunted. Its economic opportunities were limited, its standard of living increasingly impoverished. Command over credit, capital, and other scarce resources remained in white hands. The average size of black landholdings, well below fifty acres even in the 1880s, declined from year to year as lands were divided and subdivided among family members. By the 1920s, holdings of only two to four acres were common, and while many black farmers appear to have attained a modest but not uncomfortable standard of living and enjoyed a degree of autonomy unknown elsewhere in the South, the low country as a whole had become a byword for poverty, malnutrition, and economic underdevelopment.[57]

Was the success of the low-country freedmen in their struggle for the land, then, a Pyrrhic victory? Perhaps, instead, it should be viewed as a particularly dramatic illustration of the ambiguity of historical outcomes, especially the outcome of emancipation. Thinking of an entirely different experience, the English socialist William Morris reflected on how historical struggles never seem to reach a definitive conclusion: "I pondered all these things, . . . how men fight and lose the battle, and the thing that they fought for comes about in spite of their defeat, and when it comes turns out not to be what they meant, and other men have to fight for what they meant under another name."[58]

Today, the Sea Islands are crowded with luxury resorts, the playgrounds of presidents. The fine plantations of the mainland low country survive only as parks or hunting preserves.[59] And descendants of the rice workers inhabit the decaying urban ghettoes of New York and Philadelphia. In our racial institutions and attitudes, and the social dislocations around us, the unresolved legacy of emancipation is a part of our world, more than a century after the demise of slavery. And, under other names, the struggle unleashed by emancipation, for equality in social relations, access to the resources of the earth, and the fruits of one's labor, still continues.

NOTES

INTRODUCTION

1. C. Vann Woodward, "The Price of Freedom," in *What Was Freedom's Price?*, ed. David L. Sansing (Jackson, Miss., 1978), 93. For an assessment of recent work in comparative history and various definitions of the genre, see George M. Fredrickson, "Comparative History," in *The Past Before Us*, ed. Michael Kammen (Ithaca, 1980), 457–73.

2. Edgar T. Thompson, *Plantation Societies, Race Relations, and the South: The Regimentation of Populations* (Durham, 1975), 98–99.

3. On the transition from slave to free labor in the sugar region, see J. Carlyle Sitterson, *Sugar Country* (Lexington, 1953), and Joseph P. Reidy, "Sugar and Freedom: Emancipation in Louisiana's Sugar Parishes," paper, American Historical Association annual meeting, 1980.

4. The Northern response to emancipation is discussed in Eric Foner, *Politics and Ideology in the Age of the Civil War* (New York, 1980), Chaps. 6 and 7. My history of Reconstruction will appear in Harper and Row's "New American Nation" series.

5. W. E. B. Du Bois, *Black Reconstruction in America* (New York, 1935), 15.

6. Du Bois's death in 1963 was noted in the *American Historical Review* in an obituary one sentence in length. [LXIX (January, 1964), 601–602.] As every reader of that journal knows, scholars of lesser achievement have received far more extensive obituaries.

7. Mary Wilkin (ed.), "Some Papers of the American Cotton Planters' Association, 1865–1866," *Tennessee Historical Quarterly*, VIII (March, 1949), 49–50.

8. For a discussion of recent literature on Reconstruction, see my "Reconstruction Revisited," *Reviews in American History*, X (December, 1982), 82–100.

9. *Report of the Committee of the Senate Upon the Relations Between Labor and Capital, and Testimony Taken by the Committee* (4 vols.; Washington, 1885), IV, 605.

CHAPTER I

1. Thaddeus Stevens to Charles Sumner, October 7, 1865, in Charles Sumner Papers, Houghton Library, Harvard University; *Congressional Globe*, 39th Cong., 1st Sess., 658, 40th Cong., 1st Sess., 205.

2. Terence Emmons, *The Russian Landed Gentry and the Peasant Emancipation of 1861* (Cambridge, 1968), 421; Jerome Blum, *Lord and Peasant in Russia from the Ninth to the Nineteenth Century* (Princeton, 1961), 590–98; Daniel Chirot, "The Growth of the Market and Servile Labor Systems in Agriculture," *Journal of Social History*, VIII (Winter, 1975), 73; Alexander Gerschenkron, *Continuity in History and Other Essays* (Cambridge, Mass., 1968), 164–83.

3. Edgar T. Thompson, *Plantation Societies, Race Relations, and the South: The Regimentation of Populations* (Durham, 1975), 55, 70. Cf. L. A. Best, "A Model of a Pure Plantation Economy," *Social and Economic Studies*, XVII (September, 1968), 287; Sheldon Van Auken, "A Century of the Southern Plantation," *Virginia Magazine of History and Biography*, LVIII (July, 1950), 356–57; "Editorial Prospectus," *Plantation Society in the Americas*, I (February, 1979), 4–6.

4. C. L. R. James, *The Black Jacobins* (New York, 1963 ed.); Robert K. Lacerte, "The Evolution of Land and Labor in the Haitian Revolution, 1791–1820," *The Americas*, XXXIV (April, 1978), 449–59; George Tyson (ed.), *Toussaint L'Ouverture* (Englewood Cliffs, 1973), 17–20, 51–56; James G. Leyburn, *The Haitian People* (New Haven, 1941), 34–75, 320; Eugene D. Genovese, *From Rebellion to Revolution* (Baton Rouge, 1979), 88, 123–24; David Nicholls, *From Dessalines to Duvalier* (Cambridge, 1979), 29–69; Mats Lundahl, *Peasants and Poverty, a Study of Haiti* (New York, 1979). Strictly speaking, emancipation in certain parts of the northern United States (Pennsylvania and Massachusetts most notably) preceded that in Haiti, but the numbers involved were quite small.

5. David Brion Davis, *The Problem of Slavery in the Age of Revolution, 1770–1823* (Ithaca, 1975), 81; Hans Schmidt, *The United States Occupation of Haiti, 1915–1934* (New Brunswick, 1971), 24–30.

6. Schmidt, *U.S. Occupation of Haiti*, 11–12, 69, 170–83; Melvin M. Knight, *The Americans in Santo Domingo* (New York, 1928), 173; Leyburn, *Haitian People*, 96; Arthur C. Millspaugh, *Haiti Under American Control, 1915–1930* (Boston, 1931), 15.

7. William A. Green, *British Slave Emancipation: The Sugar Colonies and the Great Experiment, 1830–1865* (Oxford, 1976), 121.

8. Green, *British Slave Emancipation*, 13, 193; Stanley L. Engerman

and David Eltis, "Economic Aspects of the Abolition Debate," in *Anti-Slavery, Religion, and Reform*, ed. Christine Bolt and Seymour Drescher (Folkestone, 1980), 285–86; Stanley L. Engerman, "Economic Aspects of the Adjustments to Emancipation in the United States and the British West Indies," (MS, 1981), 5–7. There is a critique of the land/labor ratio as the key to the postemancipation adjustment in O. Nigel Bolland, "Systems of Domination After Slavery: The Control of Land and Labor in the British West Indies After 1838," *Comparative Studies in Society and History*, XXIII (October, 1981), 593.

9. Peter Mathias, *The Transformation of England* (London, 1979), 137–60; Joyce Appleby, "Ideology and Theory: The Tension Between Political and Economic Liberalism in Seventeenth-Century England," *American Historical Review*, LXXXI (June, 1976), 514–15; A. W. Coats, "Changing Attitudes to Labour in the Mid-Eighteenth Century," *Economic History Review*, 2nd ser., XI (August, 1958), 35–51.

10. Syed Hussein Alatas, *The Myth of the Lazy Native* (London, 1977); Philip D. Curtin, *The Image of Africa: British Ideas and Actions, 1780–1850* (Madison, 1964), 61–62, 251.

11. Thomas C. Holt, "'An Empire over the Mind': Emancipation, Race, and Ideology in the British West Indies and the American South," in *Race, Region, and Reconstruction: Essays in Honor of C. Vann Woodward*, ed. J. Morgan Kousser and James B. McPherson (New York, 1982), 288–89; Green, *British Slave Emancipation*, 121–22; Graham Knox, "British Colonial Policy and the Problems of Establishing a Free Society in Jamaica, 1838–1865," *Caribbean Studies*, II (January, 1963), 3.

12. Howard Temperley, *British Antislavery, 1833–1870* (London, 1972), 30.

13. Anton V. Long, *Jamaica and the New Order, 1827–1847* (Mona, Jamaica, 1956), 30–31; W. L. Burn, *Emancipation and Apprenticeship in the British West Indies* (London, 1937), 196, 203–15, 265–66.

14. Douglas Hall, *Five of the Leewards, 1834–1870* (St. Laurence, Barbados, 1971), 24; C. Vann Woodward, "The Price of Freedom," in *What Was Freedom's Price?*, ed. David L. Sansing (Jackson, Miss., 1978), 102–104; Burn, *Emancipation and Apprenticeship*, 167; Alan H. Adamson, "The Reconstruction of Plantation Labor after Emancipation: The Case of British Guiana," in *Race and Slavery in the Western Hemisphere: Quantitative Studies*, ed. Stanley L. Engerman and Eugene D. Genovese (Princeton, 1975), 460–61.

15. Bolland, "Systems of Domination," 594–95; Green, *British Slave Emancipation*, 131; Richard Frucht, "From Slavery to Unfreedom in the Plantation Society of St. Kitts, W. I.," in *Comparative Perspectives on Slavery in New World Plantation Societies*, ed. Vera Rubin and Arthur Tuden (New York, 1977), 384–86; Temperley, *British Antislavery*, 30–41.

16. W. Emanuel Riviere, "Labor Shortage in the British West Indies

After Emancipation," *Journal of Caribbean History*, IV (May, 1972), 3–4, sees the flight from the estates as reflecting blacks' definition of freedom as removing themselves from the plantations. The flight as a response to planter actions after the end of slavery is stressed in Knox, "British Colonial Policy," 7–8; Woodville K. Marshall, "Commentary," *Historical Reflections*, VI (Summer, 1979), 246–47; Douglas Hall, "The Flight from the Estates Reconsidered: The British West Indies, 1838–42," *Journal of Caribbean History*, X–XI (1978), 7–24.

17. Sidney Mintz, "Was the Plantation Slave a Proletarian?", *Review*, II (Summer, 1978), 93–94; Mintz, "Slavery and the Rise of Peasantries," *Historical Reflections*, VI (Summer, 1979), 213–42. This latter article is indispensable for an understanding of postemancipation developments in the Caribbean.

18. Philip D. Curtin, *Two Jamaicas* (Cambridge, Mass., 1955), 128–29; Hall, "Flight from the Estates," 16–21; A. J. G. Knox, "Opportunities and Opposition: The Rise of Jamaica's Black Peasantry and the Nature of Planter Resistance," *Canadian Review of Sociology and Anthropology*, XIV (November, 1977), 387; Alan H. Adamson, *Sugar Without Slaves: The Political Economy of British Guiana, 1838–1904* (New Haven, 1972), 35; Adamson, "Reconstruction of Plantation Labor," 462.

19. Knox, "Opportunities and Opposition," 385–87; Gisella Eisner, *Jamaica, 1830–1930: A Study in Economic Growth* (Manchester, Eng., 1961), 118–19, 168–70.

20. Marshall, "Commentary," 245; George L. Beckford, *Persistent Poverty: Underdevelopment in Plantation Economies of the Third World* (New York, 1972), 22; Donald Wood, *Trinidad in Transition* (London, 1968), 49–51; Riviere, "Labor Shortage in British West Indies," 10–14; Woodville K. Marshall, "Notes on Peasant Development in the West Indies Since 1838," *Social and Economic Studies*, XVII (Summer, 1968), 256; Walter Rodney, *A History of the Guyanese Working People, 1881–1905* (Baltimore, 1981), 61; Adamson, *Sugar Without Slaves*, 31–40.

21. Hall, "Flight from the Estates," 18; Marshall, "Notes on Peasant Development," 253–61; Riviere, "Labor Shortage in British West Indies," 17–23; Hall, *Five of the Leewards*, 45; Wood, *Trinidad in Transition*, 7.

22. Adamson, *Sugar Without Slaves*, 37; Douglas Hall, *Free Jamaica, 1838–1865: An Economic History* (New Haven, 1959), 166–67; Green, *British Slave Emancipation*, 194–96; Hall, *Five of the Leewards*, 30–33; Michael Craton, *Searching for the Invisible Man: Slaves and Plantation Life in Jamaica* (Cambridge, Mass., 1978), 24, 289–93.

23. Walter Rodney, "Slavery and Underdevelopment," *Historical Reflections*, VI (Summer, 1979), 284; Stanley L. Engerman, "Servants to Slaves to Servants: Contract Labor and European Expansion" (MS, 1982);

Adamson, "Reconstruction of Plantation Labor," 466–69; Wood, *Trinidad in Transition*, 119–21; Adamson, *Sugar Without Slaves*, 41–46.

24. Green, *British Slave Emancipation*, 261; Howard Johnson, "Immigration and the Sugar Industry in Trinidad During the Last Quarter of the 19th Century," *Journal of Caribbean History*, III (November, 1971), 28; Adamson, *Sugar Without Slaves*, 10; Rodney, *Guyanese Working People*, xxii.

25. Hugh Tinker, *A New System of Slavery: The Export of Indian Labour Overseas, 1830–1920* (London, 1974); Sidney W. Mintz, *Caribbean Transformations* (Chicago, 1974), 73; Beckford, *Persistent Poverty*, 101; W. Kloosterboer, *Involuntary Labor Since the Abolition of Slavery* (Leiden, 1960), 8–14, 32–33; Peter F. Klarén, "The Social and Economic Consequences of Modernization in the Peruvian Sugar Industry, 1870–1930," in *Land and Labour in Latin America*, ed. Kenneth Duncan and Ian Rutledge (Cambridge, 1977), 241–43; Ronald Takaki, "'An Entering Wedge': The Origins of the Sugar Plantation and a Multiethnic Working Class in Hawaii," *Labor History*, XXIII (Winter, 1982), 32–46.

26. Brian W. Blouet, "The Post-Emancipation Origins of the Relationships between the Estates and the Peasantry in Trinidad," in *Land and Labour in Latin America*, ed. Duncan and Rutledge, 435; Hall, *Five of the Leewards*, 150–51; Adamson, *Sugar Without Slaves*, 79; William G. Sewell, *The Ordeal of Free Labor in the British West Indies* (New York, 1861), 35–38; Green, *British Slave Emancipation*, 72–73, 176.

27. Curtin, *Two Jamaicas*, 43–44, 179–89; Knox, "Opportunities and Opposition," 388; Hall, *Free Jamaica*, 2–3, 177.

28. Temperley, *British Antislavery*, 121–22; Adamson, *Sugar Without Slaves*, 239; Knox, "Opportunities and Opposition," 392–93; Rodney, *Guyanese Working People*, xxiii; Green, *British Slave Emancipation*, 175, 188.

29. Curtin, *Two Jamaicas*, 130; Eisner, *Jamaica*, 366–68; Knox, "British Colonial Policy," 389–90; Marshall, "Notes on Peasant Development," 255; Riviere, "Labor Shortage in British West Indies," 25.

30. Wood, *Trinidad in Transition*, 7; Rodney, *Guyanese Working People*, 9–17; Knox, "Opportunities and Opposition," 391; Adamson, *Sugar Without Slaves*, 32–33, 57–77, 243; Eisner, *Jamaica*, 213; Green, *British Slave Emancipation*, 216.

31. Adamson, *Sugar Without Slaves*, 79; Rodney, *Guyanese Working People*, 128; Gad J. Heuman, *Between Black and White: Race, Politics, and the Free Coloreds in Jamaica, 1792–1865* (Westport, 1981), 64–67, 130–31; Green, *British Slave Emancipation*, 321; Marshall, "Commentary," 245; Hall, *Free Jamaica*, 8, 263; Knox, "Opportunities and Opposition," 382.

32. Marietta Morrissey, "Towards a Theory of West Indian Economic Development," *Latin American Perspectives*, VIII (Winter, 1981), 14; Hall, *Free Jamaica*, 237–56; Douglas A. Lorimer, *Colour, Class and*

the Victorians (Leicester, 1978), 179; Knox, "Opportunities and Opposition," 382–83; Hall, *Five of the Leewards*, 175–77.

33. Henry Taylor, *Autobiography of Henry Taylor, 1800–1875* (2 vols.; London, 1885), I, 247–55; Adamson, *Sugar Without Slaves*, 52; Green, *British Slave Emancipation*, 164–69; Curtin, *Two Jamaicas*, 98; Long, *Jamaica and the New Order*, 33–42.

34. Green, *British Slave Emancipation*, 84–90, 170–75; Hall, *Free Jamaica*, 179; Adamson, "Reconstruction of Plantation Labor," 458–59; Knox, "British Colonial Policy," 4–12; Knox, "Opportunities and Opposition," 381–84; Hall, *Five of the Leewards*, 153–55; Blouet, "Post-Emancipation Origins," 436–38; Taylor, *Autobiography*, I, 262–63.

35. Seymour Drescher (ed.), *Tocqueville and Beaumont on Social Reform* (New York, 1968), 117, 130–31, 166.

36. Granville J. Chester, *Transatlantic Sketches* (London, 1869), 64; Christine Bolt, *The Anti-Slavery Movement and Reconstruction* (London, 1969), 17–18, 36–43; Bernard Semmel, *Jamaican Blood and Victorian Conscience: The Governor Eyre Controversy* (London, 1962); Green, *British Slave Emancipation*, 401–402; Lorimer, *Colour, Class and the Victorians*, 123–29, 180–82; Christine Bolt, *Victorian Attitudes to Race* (London, 1971), 102–103.

37. H. J. Perkin, "Land Reform and Class Conflict in Victorian Britain," in *The Victorians and Social Protest*, ed. J. Butt and I. F. Clark (Hamden, Ct., 1973), 177–217; Clive J. Dewey, "The Rehabilitation of the Peasant Proprietor in Nineteenth-Century Economic Thought," *History of Political Economy*, VI (1974), 17–47.

38. Bolt, *Victorian Attitudes to Race*, 88–100, 209–15.

39. In the past decade there has been a remarkable renaissance in studies of the origins of modern racial and labor systems in southern Africa. An earlier body of literature, viewing the problem through the lens of "race relations," has been challenged and to a considerable extent superceded by newer work stressing how racial systems evolved in response to an exceptional demand for labor created by the expansion of capitalism and European settlement. Among the issues still being debated are: was the "peasant" a backward-looking drag on economic growth, or a farmer highly responsive to market conditions, whose decline was the result of conscious state intervention; and, did European investment break down traditional barriers to economic development, or create underdevelopment by molding the economy to the needs of the imperial relationship? Much of the recent literature derives its approach from the seminal article by Giovanni Arrighi, "Labor Supplies in Historical Perspective: A Study in the Proletarianization of the African Peasantry in Rhodesia," *Journal of Development Studies*, VI (April, 1970), 197–234. Also extremely influential has been Harold Wolpe, "Capitalism and Cheap Labor Power in South Africa: From Segregation to Apartheid," *Economy and Society*, I (November, 1972), 425–56. For reviews

of this literature, see John W. Cell, *The Highest Stage of White Supremacy: The Origins of Segregation in South Africa and the American South* (New York, 1982), Chap. 3; Ralph Austen, "Capitalism, Class and African Colonial Agriculture: The Mating of Marxism and Empiricism," *Journal of Economic History*, XLI (September, 1981), 657–63; Frederick Cooper, "Peasants, Capitalists and Historians: A Review Article," *Journal of Southern African Studies*, VII (April, 1981), 285–314. Among the signal contributions of this recent literature is that it treats Africans as historical actors rather than simply objects of white policy, a problem which mars George M. Fredrickson's otherwise exemplary *White Supremacy: A Comparative Study in American and South African History* (New York, 1981).

40. Colin Bundy, *The Rise and Fall of the South African Peasantry* (London, 1979); Arrighi, "Labor Supplies," 200–203; Frederick A. Johnstone, *Class, Race and Gold* (London, 1976), 29; Freda Troup, *South Africa: An Historical Introduction* (London, 1975), 159, 197; and the articles by Colin Bundy, Robin Palmer, Ian Phiminster, Martin Legassick, and Laurel Van Horn in *The Roots of Rural Poverty in Central and Southern Africa*, ed. Robin Palmer and Neil Parsons (London, 1977).

41. Frederick Cooper, *From Slaves to Squatters: Plantation Labor and Agriculture in Zanzibar and Coastal Kenya, 1890–1925* (New Haven, 1980), 28–30, 37–38; Anthony Clayton and Donald C. Savage, *Government and Labor in Kenya, 1895–1963* (London, 1974), xiv, 21–28, 41; Robert I. Rotberg, *A Political History of Tropical Africa* (New York, 1965), 306–307; Arrighi, "Labor Supplies," 208–10. On Britain's "abdication from the responsibility she had carried—mostly intermittently and half-heartedly, but acknowledged . . . for the interests of the Africans," see Troup, *South Africa*, 191.

42. R. M. A. Van Zwanenberg, *Colonial Capitalism and Labour in Kenya, 1919–1939* (Nairobi, 1975), 76–84; Bundy, *Rise and Fall*, 129; Arrighi, "Labor Supplies," 211–12; Cooper, "Peasants, Capitalists and Historians," 305–306; Ian Phiminster, "Peasant Production and Underdevelopment in Southern Rhodesia, 1890–1914, with Particular Reference to the Victoria District," in *Roots of Rural Poverty*, ed. Palmer and Parsons, 260–64. Laurel Van Horn, "The Agricultural History of Barotseland, 1840–1964," in *Roots of Rural Poverty*, ed. Palmer and Parsons, 151, notes the irony that one reason for the abolition of slavery in Barotseland in 1907 was dissatisfaction among Rhodesian mine owners over the limited size of the labor force produced by taxation. They concluded that slavery was the cause and forced Africans to abolish the institution. On the general relationship of taxation and peasantries, see Murdo J. MacLeod, "The Sociological Theory of Taxation and the Peasant," *Peasant Studies Newsletter*, IV (July, 1975), 2–6.

43. Monica Wilson and Leonard Thompson, (eds.), *The Oxford History of South Africa* (2 vols.; Oxford, 1969–1971), II, 127–30; Johnstone,

Class, Race and Gold, 23–24; Van Zwanenberg, *Colonial Capitalism and Labour,* 183–91, 210–12; Clayton and Savage, *Government and Labor,* 32, 43; Cooper, *Slaves to Squatters,* 116, 237; Martin Legassick, "Gold, Agriculture, and Secondary Industry in South Africa, 1885–1970," in *Roots of Rural Poverty,* ed. Palmer and Parsons, 179–82.

44. Cooper, *Slaves to Squatters,* 90–92, 203–204; Cooper, "Peasants, Capitalists and Historians," 299–301; J. K. Rennie, "White Farmers, Black Tenants and Landlord Legislation: Southern Rhodesia, 1890–1930," *Journal of Southern African Studies,* V (October, 1978), 87–89; Tim Keegan, "The Restructuring of Agrarian Class Relations in a Colonial Economy: The Orange River Colony, 1902–1910," *Journal of Southern African Studies,* V (April, 1979), 236–37; John Lonsdale and Bruce Berman, "Coping with the Contradictions: The Development of the Colonial State in Kenya, 1895–1914," *Journal of African History,* XX (1979), 494–96, 504; Robin Palmer, *Land and Racial Domination in Rhodesia* (Berkeley, 1977), 13, 57, 71–73, 80–81, 132–36. On forced labor, see Kloosterboer, *Involuntary Labor,* 162–64; Chirot, "Growth of the Market," 71–72; Cooper, *Slaves to Squatters,* 268; and W. G. Clarence-Smith, *Slaves, Peasants and Capitalists in Southern Angola, 1850–1926* (Cambridge, 1979), which stresses (p. 53) that "access to state power was fundamental to the whole labour question" in Angola, but adds that, since there was only a small class of white settlers in this Portuguese colony, peasant production persisted despite the creation of a dependent migrant labor force. Similarly, in British and French West Africa, which lacked a white settler society, colonial authorities preferred to cooperate with export-oriented African peasants rather than seeking to create a wage labor force. A. G. Hopkins, *An Economic History of West Africa* (London, 1973), 170, 211–14.

45. Kit S. Taylor, *Sugar and the Underdevelopment of Northeastern Brazil, 1500–1970* (Gainesville, 1978), 58.

46. Kenneth H. Parsons, "Land Reform in the Postwar Era," *Land Economics,* XXXIII (August, 1957), 215–16; James F. Petras and Robert LaPorte, Jr., *Cultivating Revolution: The United States and Agrarian Reform in Latin America* (New York, 1971), 19–20; Peter Dorner, *Land Reform and Economic Development* (London, 1972), 19; David Lehman (ed.), *Agrarian Reform and Agrarian Reformism* (London, 1974), 271, 297–98; Philip M. Raup, "Land Reform and Agricultural Development," in *Agricultural Development and Economic Growth,* ed. Herman W. Southworth and Bruce F. Johnson (Ithaca, 1967), 290–91; Alain de Janvry and Carlos Garramón, "The Dynamics of Rural Poverty in Latin America," *Journal of Peasant Studies,* IV (April, 1977), 99–102. Not all these works deal with the same phenomena: "agrarian reform" covers a multitude of programs, benefits, and sins, ranging from minor changes in agricultural practices to drastic redistributions of land. It is advocated by some to preserve political stability and the existing economic order,

by others as part of a revolutionary transformation of society. See the discussions in Lehman (ed.), *Agrarian Reform*, 13–22; James Petras, *Politics and Social Structure in Latin America* (New York, 1970), 250–53.

47. On "articulation" in a number of historical contexts, see Alan Richards, "The Political Economy of *Gutwirtschaft*: A Comparative Analysis of East Elbian Germany, Egypt, and Chile," *Comparative Studies in Society and History*, XXI (October, 1979), 484–86; Robert Brenner, "The Origins of Capitalist Development: A Critique of Neo-Smithian Marxism," *New Left Review*, 104 (July–August, 1977), 25; Lonsdale and Berman, "Coping with the Contradictions," 487–89; Palmer and Parsons (eds.), *Roots of Rural Poverty*, 4–5; Cooper, "Peasants, Capitalists and Historians," 286–87; Michael Taussig, "Peasant Economics and the Development of Capitalist Agriculture in the Cauca Valley, Colombia," *Latin American Perspectives*, V (Summer, 1978), 67.

48. Hall, *Five of the Leewards*, 45; Raup, "Land Reform and Agricultural Development," 297–304; Elias H. Tuma, "Agrarian Reform in Historical Perspective Revisited," *Comparative Studies in Society and History*, XXI (January, 1979), 25–29.

49. Cooper, *Slaves to Squatters*, 121–22, 153; Cooper, "Peasants, Capitalists and Historians," 303–304; Richards, "Political Economy of *Gutwertschaft*," 518; Beckford, *Persistent Poverty*, 23–28, 180–81.

50. Drescher (ed.), *Tocqueville and Beaumont*, 167; Adamson, *Sugar Without Slaves*, 10; Beckford, *Persistent Poverty*, 102–15; Harry Bernstein and Michael Pitt, "Plantations and Modes of Production," *Journal of Peasant Studies*, I (July, 1974), 516–17; Stanley B. Greenberg, *Race and State in Capitalist Development: Comparative Perspectives* (New Haven, 1980), 26–27.

51. Karl Marx and Frederick Engels, *Selected Works* (2 vols.; Moscow, 1962), I, 247.

52. Beckford, *Persistent Poverty* has been criticized for its stress on continuity in plantation societies. An application of the theory of plantation society to the United States, revealing its tendency to an ahistorical denial of substantive change is found in Jay R. Mandle, *The Roots of Black Poverty: The Southern Plantation Economy After the Civil War* (Durham, 1978). For critiques of the theory of "plantation society," see Morrissey, "West Indian Economic Development," and Riva Berleant-Schiller, "Plantation Society and the Caribbean Present: History, Anthropology and the Plantation," *Plantation Society in the Americas*, I (October, 1981), 387–409.

53. I have also found the following accounts on emancipation and its consequences, not already cited, valuable in conceptualizing the process as a whole: the numerous articles in Kenneth Duncan and Ian Rutledge (eds.), *Land and Labor in Latin America*; Stanley J. Stein, *Vassouras, A Brazilian Coffee County, 1850–1900* (Cambridge, Mass., 1957), 259–84; Thomas H. Holloway, *Immigrants on the Land: Coffee*

and Society in São Paolo, 1886–1934 (Chapel Hill, 1980); Peter L. Eisenberg, *The Sugar Industry in Pernambuco: Modernization Without Change, 1840–1910* (Berkeley, 1974); Arnold J. Bauer, "Rural Workers in Spanish America: Problems of Peonage and Oppression," *Hispanic American Historical Review*, LIX (February, 1979), 34–63; Patrick Bryan, "The Transition of Plantation Agriculture in the Dominican Republic, 1870–84," *Journal of Caribbean History*, X–XI (1978), 82–105; Rebecca J. Scott, "Postemancipation Adaptations in Cuba, 1880–1899," paper, American Historical Association annual meeting, December, 1981.

CHAPTER II

1. C. Vann Woodward, "The Price of Freedom," in *What Was Freedom's Price?*, ed. David L. Sansing (Jackson, Miss., 1978), 95–97; Lawrence N. Powell, *New Masters: Northern Planters During the Civil War and Reconstruction* (New Haven, 1980), xi–xii; *Congressional Globe*, 39th Cong., 2nd Sess., Appendix, 78.

2. Douglass Adair, *Fame and the Founding Fathers*, ed. Trevor Colbourn (New York, 1974), 108–109.

3. Winthrop D. Jordan, *White Over Black* (Chapel Hill, 1968), 378–86; William W. Freehling, *Prelude to Civil War: The Nullification Controversy in South Carolina, 1816–1836* (New York, 1966), 16; Joe B. Wilkins, Jr., "Window on Freedom: The South's Response to the Emancipation of the Slaves in the British West Indies, 1833–1861" (Ph.D. dissertation, University of South Carolina, 1977); Eric L. McKitrick (ed.), *Slavery Defended: The Views of the Old South* (Englewood Cliffs, 1963), 49.

4. Louis B. Filler, *The Crusade Against Slavery, 1830–1860* (New York, 1960), 140; William G. Sewell, *The Ordeal of Free Labor in the British West Indies* (New York, 1861), 56; James M. McPherson, "Was West Indian Emancipation a Success? The Abolitionist Argument during the American Civil War," *Caribbean Studies*, IV (July, 1964), 28–34.

5. Eugene D. Genovese, *From Rebellion to Revolution* (Baton Rouge, 1979), 95–97; Willard B. Gatewood, Jr., *Black Americans and the White Man's Burden, 1898–1903* (Urbana, 1975), 11–12; Robert Starobin (ed.), *Denmark Vesey* (Englewood Cliffs, 1970), 48; Philip S. Foner (ed.), *The Life and Writings of Frederick Douglass* (4 vols.; New York, 1950–55), IV, 478–90; Howard H. Bell (ed.), *Black Separatism and the Caribbean, 1860* (Ann Arbor, 1970), passim.

6. Edward Atkinson, *On Cotton* (Boston, 1865), 36; Sara Forbes Hughes (ed.), *Letters (Supplementary) of John Murray Forbes* (3 vols.; Boston, 1905), III, 44–45, 59; Lydia Maria Child to Charles Sumner, November 27, 1865, in Charles Sumner Papers, Houghton Library, Harvard University; Harold Hyman (ed.), *The Radical Republicans and Recon-*

struction (Indianapolis, 1967), 301–302; Lydia Maria Child, *The Freedmen's Book* (Boston, 1869), 52–55.

7. Forrest G. Wood, *Black Scare: The Racist Response to Emancipa-
tion* (Berkeley, 1968), 121; Claude H. Nolen, *The Negro's Image in the
South* (Lexington, 1967), 23; Dan T. Carter, "Fateful Legacy: White
Southerners and the Dilemma of Emancipation," *Proceedings*, South
Carolina Historical Association, 1977, pp. 49–63; New York *World*, July
29, 1865.

8. Lewis Malone Ayres to D. H. Jacques, December 26, 1865, in
Lewis Malone Ayres Papers, South Caroliniana Library, University of
South Carolina; Carter, "Fateful Legacy," 54–55; John H. Moore (ed.),
The Juhl Letters to the 'Charleston Courier' (Athens, 1974), 69–70; *Me-
morial from the Cotton Planters' Convention, Which Met in Macon,
Sept. 6, 1866* (Macon, 1866), 4; Louisville *Democrat*, quoted in Colum-
bia, S.C., *Daily Phoenix*, August 3, 1866.

9. Edgar T. Thompson, *Plantation Societies, Race Relations, and
the South: The Regimentation of Populations* (Durham, 1975), 69, 85,
98–99; Elizabeth G. McPherson (ed.), "Letters from North Carolina to
Andrew Johnson," *North Carolina Historical Review*, XXVII (October,
1950), 477.

10. Sir Frederick Bruce to Earl of Clarendon, December 12, 1865, in
Clarendon Deposit, Bodleian Library, University of Oxford; Charles
Stearns, *The Black Man of the South, and the Rebels* (New York, 1872),
339; F. W. Loring and C. F. Atkinson, *Cotton Culture and the South*
(Boston, 1869), 13, 92. Desire for land is termed "irrational" in Joseph D.
Reid, "Sharecropping as an Understandable Market Response—the Post-
Bellum South," *Journal of Economic History*, XXXIII (March, 1973), 124.

11. Frederick Cooper, *From Slaves to Squatters: Plantation Labor
and Agriculture in Zanzibar and Coastal Kenya, 1890–1925* (New
Haven, 1980), 278; Joseph P. Reidy, "Masters and Slaves, Planters and
Freedmen: The Transition from Slavery to Freedom in Central Georgia,
1820–1880" (Ph.D. dissertation, Northern Illinois University, 1982),
180; William H. Trescot to [?], February 9, 1866 (typescript), in William
H. Trescot Papers, South Caroliniana Library, University of South
Carolina.

12. Jonathan Wiener, *Social Origins of the New South, 1860–1885*
(Baton Rouge, 1978); Ronald L. F. Davis, "Labor Dependency Among
Freedmen, 1865–1880," in *From Old South to New: Essays on the Tran-
sitional South*, ed. Walter J. Fraser, Jr. and Winfred B. Moore (Westport,
1981), 155–65; Selma, Ala., *Southern Argus*, March 17, 1870; Gavin
Wright, *The Political Economy of the Cotton South* (New York, 1978),
162; Arnold J. Bauer, "Rural Workers in Spanish America: Problems of
Peonage and Oppression," *Hispanic American Historical Review*, LIX
(February, 1979), 41.

13. *Rural Carolinian*, I (February, 1870), 317; *Southern Field and*

Factory, I (January 1871), 15; Loring and Atkinson, *Cotton Culture,* 30, 32; *Congressional Globe,* 43rd Cong., 2nd Sess., Appendix, 67.

14. Douglas A. Lorimer, *Colour, Class and the Victorians* (Leicester, 1978), 15; *Congressional Globe,* 43rd Cong., 1st Sess., 416.

15. Gilbert C. Fite, "Southern Agriculture Since the Civil War: An Overview," *Agricultural History,* LIII (January, 1979), 9–10; Paul M. Gaston, *The New South Creed* (New York, 1970), 65–66; *Rural Carolinian,* I (November, 1869), 71; Stephen J. DeCanio, *Agriculture in the Postbellum South: The Economics of Production and Supply* (Cambridge, Mass., 1974), 3; Columbia, S.C., *Daily Phoenix,* April 17, 1868.

16. Rowland T. Berthoff, "Southern Attitudes Toward Immigration, 1865–1914," *Journal of Southern History,* XVII (August, 1951), 328–37; Willard Range, *A Century of Georgia Agriculture, 1850–1950* (Athens, 1954), 80; William E. Highsmith, "Louisiana Landholding During War and Reconstruction," *Louisiana Historical Quarterly,* XXXVIII (January, 1955), 44–45; William W. Davis, *The Civil War and Reconstruction in Florida* (New York, 1913), 451–52; A. B. Cooper to Governor Robert M. Patton, May 25, 1867, in Alabama Governor's Papers, Alabama State Department of Archives and History; Robert A. Gilmour, "The Other Emancipation: Studies in the Society and Economy of Alabama Whites During Reconstruction" (Ph.D. dissertation, Johns Hopkins University, 1972), 41.

17. J. G. deRoulhac Hamilton (ed.), *The Papers of Thomas Ruffin* (4 vols.; Raleigh, 1920), IV, 45; Lucy M. Cohen, "Entry of Chinese to the Lower South from 1864 to 1870: Policy Dilemmas," *Southern Studies,* XVII (Spring, 1978), 5–38; Vernon Lane Wharton, *The Negro in Mississippi, 1865–1890* (Chapel Hill, 1947), 97–98; New York *Herald,* October 22, 1869; Robert Somers, *The Southern States Since the War, 1870–71* (London, 1871), 163, 225; James W. Loewen, *The Mississippi Chinese* (Cambridge, Mass., 1971), 1–2, 22–31; Gunther Barth, *Bitter Strength: A History of the Chinese in the United States, 1850–1870* (Cambridge, Mass., 1964), 188, 194–96.

18. William W. Rogers, *The One-Gallused Rebellion: Agrarianism in Alabama, 1865–1896* (Baton Rouge, 1970), 80; James S. Pike, *The Prostrate State* (New York, 1874), 55; David J. Hellwig, "Black Attitudes toward Immigrant Labor in the South, 1865–1910," *Filson Club Historical Quarterly,* LIV (April, 1980), 153–56; Cohen, "Entry of Chinese," 14–25.

19. Arney R. Childs (ed.), *The Private Journal of Henry William Revenal 1859–1887* (Columbia, S.C., 1947), 256; Wharton, *Negro in Mississippi,* 82–83; J. W. Throckmorton to Benjamin Epperson, August 6, 1865, in Benjamin Epperson Papers, University of Texas.

20. Highsmith, "Louisiana Landholding," 44. The Black Codes are reprinted in *Senate Executive Documents,* 39th Cong., 2nd Sess., No. 6.

21. *Senate Executive Documents,* 39th Cong., 2nd Sess., No. 6, pp.

190–97, 202–19. Theodore B. Wilson, *The Black Codes of the South* (University, Ala., 1965), 71, claims those who drew up the South Carolina laws "honestly attempted to do justice to the freedmen."

22. Wilson, *Black Codes*, 96–100; *Senate Executive Documents*, 39th Cong., 2nd Sess., No. 6, pp. 172–77, 180–83, 222–26; William Cohen, "Negro Involuntary Servitude in the South, 1865–1940: A Preliminary Analysis," *Journal of Southern History*, XLII (February 1976), 35–50; Howard N. Rabinowitz, *Race Relations in the Urban South, 1865–1890* (New York, 1978), 35.

23. *De Bow's Review*, After the War Series, II (September, 1866), 309; Columbia, S.C., *Daily Phoenix*, November 12, 1865; Daphne Simon, "Master and Servant," in *Democracy and the Labour Movement*, ed. John Saville (London, 1954), 160–200; Charles Fairman, *Reconstruction and Reunion, 1864–88: Part One* (New York, 1971), 111; John W. DuBose, *Alabama's Tragic Decade*, ed. James K. Greer (Birmingham, 1940), 55. C. J. Ribton-Turner, *A History of Vagrants and Vagrancy and Beggars and Begging* (London, 1887), details the Draconian medieval British legislation concerning vagrancy. The less stringent Vagrant Act of 1824, in force during American Reconstruction, divided vagrants into three groups: those willfully refusing to support themselves (termed "Idle and Disorderly Persons"), those repeating such an offense ("Rogues and Vagabonds"), and multiple offenders, who could be sentenced to a year in prison ("Incorrigible Rogues.")

24. W. E. B. Du Bois, *Black Reconstruction in America* (New York, 1935), 166; Wilson, *Black Codes*, 70; Wharton, *Negro in Mississippi*, 90; Daniel R. Goodloe, "History of Southern Provisional Governments of 1865" (MS in Daniel R. Goodloe Papers, Southern Historical Collection, University of North Carolina); *Congressional Globe*, 43rd Cong., 2nd Sess., Appendix, 169; Fairman, *Reconstruction and Reunion*, 114–15.

25. Eric Foner, *Politics and Ideology in the Age of the Civil War* (New York, 1980), 114; Daniel A. Novack, *The Wheel of Servitude: Black Forced Labor after Slavery* (Lexington, 1978), 22–23; *House Reports*, 42nd Cong., 2nd Sess., No. 22 (Ku Klux Klan Hearings), Florida, 101; Montgomery *Alabama State Journal*, February 10, 1871; "John" to Governor Adelbert Ames, February 9, 1874, in Mississippi Governor's Papers, Mississippi Department of Archives.

26. *Rural Carolinian*, III (March, 1872), 335; Foner, *Politics and Ideology*, 115; *Address Delivered Before the Agricultural Society of South Carolina* (Charleston, 1872), 33; Hannsboro (Miss.) *Democrat*, quoted in *Southern Field and Factory*, I (September, 1871), 304.

27. Savannah *Advertiser and Republican*, August 17, 1873; Cohen, "Negro Involuntary Servitude," 31–60; Pete Daniel, "The Metamorphosis of Slavery, 1865–1900," *Journal of American History*, LXVI (June, 1979), 88–99; Novack, *Wheel of Servitude*, passim.

28. *Senate Reports*, 46th Cong., 2nd Sess., No. 693 (Negro Exodus

Hearings), II, 219–20; Nashville *Union and American*, May 21, 1875.

29. Morton J. Horwitz, *The Transformation of American Law, 1780–1860* (Cambridge, Mass., 1977); Harry N. Scheiber, "Regulation, Property Rights, and Definition of 'The Market': Law and the American Economy," *Journal of Economic History*, XLI (March, 1981), 104.

30. Mary Wilkin (ed.), "Some Papers of the American Cotton Planters' Association, 1865–1866," *Tennessee Historical Quarterly*, VIII (March, 1949), 49–50.

31. Eugene D. Genovese, *Roll, Jordan, Roll* (New York, 1974), 535–40; John W. Blassingame (ed.), *Slave Testimony* (Baton Rouge, 1977), 393; Ira Berlin, "Time, Space, and the Evolution of Afro-American Society in British Mainland North America," *American Historical Review*, LXXXV (February, 1980), 61–66; Sam B. Hilliard, *Hog Meat and Hoecake* (Carbondale, 1972), 182–85; Roderick A. McDonald, "'Goods and Chattels': The Economy of Slaves on Sugar Plantations in Jamaica and Louisiana" (Ph.D. dissertation, University of Kansas, 1981), 113–51.

32. Henry B. Richardson to Henry and Anna Richardson, May 16, 1866, in Henry B. Richardson Papers, Louisiana State University; "Colloquy With Colored Ministers," *Journal of Negro History*, XVI (January, 1931), 91; *House Reports*, 39th Cong., 1st Sess., No. 30 (Report of the Joint Committee on Reconstruction), II, 185; Mobile *Nationalist*, May 16, 1867.

33. Bayley Wyat, *A Freedman's Speech* (Philadelphia, 1867); Elias Yulee, *An Address to the Colored People of Georgia* (Savannah, 1868), 11.

34. E. P. Thompson, *Whigs and Hunters: The Origin of the Black Act* (New York, 1975), 207; Bliss Perry, *Life and Letters of Henry Lee Higginson* (2 vols.; Boston, 1921), I, 256.

35. Kenneth M. Stampp, *The Peculiar Institution* (New York, 1956), 125; Genovese, *Roll, Jordan, Roll*, 599–609; *House Reports*, 42nd Cong., 2nd Sess., No. 22 (Ku Klux Klan Hearings), South Carolina, 167; Isaac D. Williams, *Sunshine and Shadow of Plantation Life* (East Saginaw, Mich., 1885), 58–59.

36. Edward Ayres, "The Shape of Serious Crime in the Nineteenth-Century South" (paper, Organization of American Historians annual meeting, 1982); George A. Trenholm to Alfred G. Trenholm, October 7, 1865, in George A. Trenholm Papers, South Caroliniana Library, University of South Carolina; *House Reports*, 42nd Cong., 2nd Sess., No. 22 (Ku Klux Klan Hearings), South Carolina, 121; T. Roman to [?], May 27, 1868, in Bienvenue Family Papers, Louisiana State University (original in French; translation, Lynn Garafola); D. M. Carter to Governor Tod R. Caldwell, May 19, 1872, in North Carolina Governor's Papers, North Carolina State Archives; LaWanda and John H. Cox (eds.), *Reconstruction, the Negro, and the New South* (Columbia, S.C., 1973), 278.

37. Loring and Atkinson, *Cotton Culture*, 72, 88–89; James W.

Garner, *Reconstruction in Mississippi* (New York, 1901), 307–309; *House Reports*, 42nd Cong., 2nd Sess., No. 22 (Ku Klux Klan Hearings), South Carolina, 237.

38. Beaufort, S.C., *Tribune*, May 10, 1877; Jackson *Daily Mississippi Pilot*, January 27, 1871; Jerrell H. Shofner, *Nor Is It Over Yet: Florida in the Era of Reconstruction, 1863–1877* (Gainesville, 1974), 130; Charles L. Flynn, Jr., "White Land, Black Labor: Property, Ideology, and the Political Economy of Late Nineteenth-Century Georgia" (Ph.D. dissertation, Duke University, 1980), 118–19; Allen J. Going, *Bourbon Democracy in Alabama, 1874–1890* (University, Ala., 1951), 97; *Senate Reports*, 46th Cong., 2nd Sess., No. 693 (Negro Exodus Hearings), II, 466–67.

39. Novack, *Wheel of Servitude*, 31–32; Moore (ed.), *Juhl Letters*, 59–60; Alrutheus A. Taylor, *The Negro in South Carolina During the Reconstruction* (Washington, 1924), 264; *Senate Reports*, 46th Cong., 2nd Sess., No. 693 (Negro Exodus Hearings), I, 130, II, 260–61; Wharton, *Negro in Mississippi*, 235–38.

40. *Colored Men, Read! How Your Friends are Treated!*, broadside, July, 1876, in R. C. Martin Papers, Louisiana State University; *Congressional Globe*, 43rd Cong., 1st Sess., 427; Rabinowitz, *Race Relations*, 41–43; Alwyn Barr, *Reconstruction to Reform: Texas Politics, 1876–1906* (Austin, 1971), 9; *Congressional Globe*, 39th Cong., 2nd Sess., 1709.

41. Harold D. Woodman, "Post-Civil War Southern Agriculture and the Law," *Agricultural History*, LIII (January, 1979), 319–37; LaWanda Cox and John H. Cox (eds.), *Reconstruction*, 236–40; Jerrell H. Shofner, "Militant Negro Laborers in Reconstruction Florida," *Journal of Southern History*, XXXIX (August, 1973), 408; John W. Graves, "Town and Country: Race Relations and Urban Development in Arkansas, 1865–1905" (Ph.D. dissertation, University of Virginia, 1978), 66; S. Z. Williamson to Richard Sadler, March 24, 1870, in Daniel Hope Sadler Papers, Winthrop College, Rock Hill, S.C.

42. Records of the Office of the Secretary of Agriculture, Agricultural Adjustment Administration, Legal Division, File 466 (Landlord-Tenant Relations), Record Group 16, National Archives; *Senate Reports*, 46th Cong., 2nd Sess., No. 693 (Negro Exodus Hearings), I, 209, 407; II, 413–14; Range, *Georgia Agriculture*, 85; Woodman, "Agriculture and the Law," 319–37.

43. Jean-Jacques Rousseau, *The First and Second Discourses* (New York, 1964), 141–42; J. Crawford King, "The Closing of the Southern Range: An Exploratory Study," *Journal of Southern History*, XLVIII (February, 1982), 53–54; Steven H. Hahn, "Common Rights and Commonwealth: The Stock-Law Struggle and the Roots of Southern Populism," in *Region, Race and Reconstruction: Essays in Honor of C. Vann Woodward*, ed. J. Morgan Kousser and James M. McPherson (New York, 1982),

51–88; Lewis C. Gray, *History of Agriculture in the Southern United States* (Washington, 1932), 843; *Report of the Commissioner of Agriculture for the Year 1869* (Washington, 1870), 394–410.

44. Earl W. Hayter, "Livestock-Fencing Conflicts in Rural America," *Agricultural History*, XXXVII (January, 1963), 10–20; Margaret B. Bogue, *Patterns from the Sod* (Springfield, 1959), 133–36; Allan G. Bogue, *From Prairie to Corn Belt: Farming on the Illinois and Iowa Prairies in the Nineteenth Century* (Chicago, 1963), 81–83; John Ludeke, "The No Fence Law of 1874: Victory for San Joaquin Valley Farmers," *California History*, LIX (Summer, 1980), 98–115; Barr, *Reconstruction to Reform*, 81.

45. Loring and Atkinson, *Cotton Culture*, 65–66; Forrest McDonald and Grady McWhiney, "The Antebellum Southern Herdsman: An Interpretation," *Journal of Southern History*, LI (May, 1975), 164–65; Charles Nordhoff, *The Cotton States in the Spring and Summer of 1875* (New York, 1876), 21–22, 70; W. H. Robert to Governor Daniel H. Chamberlain, December 9, 1874, in South Carolina Governor's Papers, South Carolina Archives; King, "Closing of the Southern Range," 56; *Rural Carolinian*, II (October, 1870), 37 (May, 1871), 464 (June, 1871), 516–19; *Southern Field and Factory*, I (September, 1871), 306.

46. Selma, Ala., *Southern Argus*, December 1, 1869; *Rural Carolinian*, IV (February, 1873), 232; Charleston *News and Courier*, February 10, 1876; Charleston *Daily Republican*, December 4, 1869; Savannah *Colored Tribune*, June 17, 1876; Theodore Rosengarten, *All God's Dangers: The Life of Nate Shaw* (New York, 1974), 13, 49.

47. King, "Closing of Southern Range," 57–63; Steven Hahn, "Hunting, Fishing, and Foraging: The Transformation of Property Rights in the Postbellum South," *Radical History Review*, 26 (October, 1982), 37–64; Hahn, "Common Rights and Commonwealth," 51–88; Flynn, "White Land, Black Labor," 164–74; McDonald and McWhiney, "Southern Herdsman," 157–58; J. D. Chambers and G. E. Mingay, *The Agricultural Revolution, 1750–1850* (London, 1966), 96–98.

48. Thompson, *Whigs and Hunters*, passim; Douglas Hay, "Poaching and the Game Laws on Cannock Chase," in *Albion's Fatal Tree*, ed. Douglas Hay, Peter Linebaugh, and E. P. Thompson (London, 1975), 189–92.

49. Hahn, "Hunting, Fishing, and Foraging," 41–43; John Solomon Otto, "A New Look at Slave Life," *Natural History*, LXXXVIII (January, 1979), 8–30; Flynn, "White Land, Black Labor," 156.

50. Henry Crydenwise to "Dear Parents," December 11, 1866, in Henry Crydenwise Papers, Perkins Library, Duke University; M. H. Wetson to Governor William W. Holden, October 16, 1868, in North Carolina Governor's Papers; "Reticent" to Governor Benjamin G. Humphreys, October 30, 1866, in Mississippi Governor's Papers.

51. *Senate Executive Documents*, 39th Cong., 2nd Sess., No. 6, pp.

174, 183–84, 218–19; Flynn, "White Land, Black Labor," 147–49; *Southern Field and Factory*, IV (February, 1874), 669; Edward King, *The Southern States of North America* (London, 1875), 434; W. H. Robert to Governor Daniel H. Chamberlain, December 9, 1874, in South Carolina Governor's Papers; *Senate Miscellaneous Documents*, 44th Cong., 2nd Sess., No. 45, p. 189; *House Reports*, 43rd Cong., 2nd Sess., No. 262, p. 421–23.

52. *Fur, Fin and Feather: A Compilation of the Game Laws of the Principal States* (5th ed.; New York, 1872), 58–59; Flynn, "White Land, Black Labor," 151, 161–63; Hahn, "Hunting, Fishing, and Foraging," 49–52; Joshua W. Caldwell, *Studies in the Constitutional History of Tennessee* (Cincinnati, 1895), 156. Range, *Georgia Agriculture*, 99, notes that an unlikely alliance of black voters and "fox hunters" succeeded in blocking efforts to tax dogs until the end of the nineteenth century.

53. J. Mills Thornton III, "Fiscal Policy and the Failure of Radical Reconstruction in the Lower South," in *Region, Race, and Reconstruction*, ed. Kousser and McPherson, 349–94; *House Reports*, 42nd Cong., 2nd Sess., No. 22 (Ku Klux Klan Hearings), Mississippi, 728, South Carolina, 117, 132, 775; J. M. Hollander (ed.), *Studies in State Taxation* (Baltimore, 1900), 85–86, 187; Dorothy Sterling (ed.), *The Trouble They Seen* (Garden City, 1976), 430; Peter Wallenstein, "From Slave South to New South: Taxes and Spending in Georgia from 1850 Through Reconstruction," *Journal of Economic History*, XXXVI (March, 1976), 287–90.

54. Jackson *Weekly Mississippi Pilot*, August 29, 1870, January 23, 1875; *Senate Executive Documents*, 39th Cong., 2nd Sess., No. 6, pp. 1192–93; Shofner, *Nor Is It Over*, 50–53; Lt. Col. Allan Rutherford, Annual Report, October 29, 1866, Annual Reports of Operations, North Carolina Assistant Commissioner's Office, in Record Group 105, Freedmen's Bureau Papers, National Archives. Blacks did not object to paying taxes per se—they simply insisted on receiving some benefit from the revenues raised. It was not uncommon for local black communities to tax themselves voluntarily to raise teachers' salaries. See, for example, Jane T. Shelton, *Pines and Pioneers: A History of Lowndes County, Georgia, 1825–1900* (Atlanta, 1976), 167.

55. Thornton, "Fiscal Policy"; Joel Williamson, *After Slavery: The Negro in South Carolina During Reconstruction, 1861–1877* (Chapel Hill, 1965), 150–53; *House Reports*, 42nd Cong., 2nd Sess., No. 22 (Ku Klux Klan Hearings), South Carolina, 242, 892, Georgia, 304, Mississippi, 369, 507.

56. J. G. deRoulhac Hamilton (ed.), *The Papers of Randolph Abbott Shotwell* (3 vols.; Raleigh, 1929–36), II, 284; "Anonymous" to Governor Robert K. Scott, March 13, 1871, J. M. Runion to Scott, March 25, 1871, in South Carolina Governor's Papers; Willie Lee Rose, *Rehearsal for Reconstruction: The Port Royal Experiment* (Indianapolis, 1964), 396; Eliz-

abeth H. Botume, *First Days Among the Contrabands* (Boston, 1893), 278–79; New York *Tribune*, August 1, 1872; *Senate Miscellaneous Documents*, 44th Cong., 2nd Sess., No. 48, II, 192.

57. *House Reports*, 42nd Cong., 2nd Sess., No. 22 (Ku Klux Klan Hearings), South Carolina, 238–39; David Lehman (ed.), *Agrarian Reform and Agrarian Reformism* (London, 1974), 280–81; Robert L. Brandfon, *Cotton Kingdom of the New South* (Cambridge, Mass., 1967), 41–42; Graves, "Town and Country," 151–52; Selma, Ala., *Southern Argus*, June 16, 1870; Williamson, *After Slavery*, 153–55; William C. Harris, *The Day of the Carpetbagger: Republican Reconstruction in Mississippi* (Baton Rouge, 1979), 334, 486, 507; Michael S. Wayne, "Ante-Bellum Planters in the Post-Bellum South: The Natchez District, 1860–1880" (Ph.D. dissertation, Yale University, 1979), 115–16, 135–38; J. Randall Stanley, *History of Jackson County* (Marianna, Fla., 1950), 201–202. The only full-scale study of nineteenth-century tax auctions, Robert P. Swierenga, *Acres for Cents: Delinquent Tax Auctions in Frontier Iowa* (Westport, 1976), concludes tax-buying was a form of investment, rather than land acquisition. It enabled farmers to borrow money from those who advanced funds for taxes, albeit at high interest rates. Most land was redeemed before title was permanently lost, and the courts were so ready to protect tax delinquents that it became proverbial that "a tax title is no title at all."

58. Joe Gray Taylor, *Louisiana Reconstructed, 1863–1877* (Baton Rouge, 1974), 508; Nell I. Painter, *Exodusters* (New York, 1976), 58; *Senate Reports*, 46th Cong., 2nd Sess., No. 693 (Negro Exodus Hearings), II, 219–20; *Senate Reports*, 44th Cong., 2nd Sess., No. 704, p. 137; Going, *Bourbon Democracy in Alabama*, 97; *The Weekly Sun*, August 6, 1874, clipping, in John E. Bryant Papers, Perkins Library, Duke University; Crandall A. Shifflett, *Patronage and Poverty in the Tobacco South: Louisa County, Virginia, 1860–1900* (Knoxville, 1982), Chap. 5; J. Morgan Kousser, "Progressivism—For Middle Class Whites Only: North Carolina Education, 1880–1910," *Journal of Southern History*, XLVI (May, 1980), 173.

59. Du Bois, *Black Reconstruction*, 591.

60. Wright, *Political Economy of the Cotton South*, 178; *Report of the Committee of the Senate Upon the Relations Between Labor and Capital, and Testimony Taken by the Committee* (4 vols.; Washington, 1885), IV, 542; Flynn, "White Land, Black Labor," 103; *Senate Miscellaneous Documents*, 44th Cong., 2nd Sess., No. 48, I, 473.

CHAPTER III

1. *Congressional Record*, 44th Cong., 2nd Sess., Appendix, 256.

2. Lewis C. Gray, *History of Agriculture in the Southern United States* (Washington, 1932), 721–28; Charles W. Joyner, "Slave Folklife on the Waccamaw Neck: Antebellum Black Culture in the South Car-

olina Lowcountry," (Ph.D. dissertation, Folklore and Folklife, University of Pennsylvania, 1977), 2–4, 46–47; James M. Clifton (ed.), *Life and Labor on Argyle Island* (Savannah, 1978), viii–xiii; Edward King, *The Southern States of North America* (London, 1875), 434–35; James M. Clifton, "A Half-Century of a Georgia Rice Plantation," *North Carolina Historical Review*, XLVII (Autumn, 1970), 388–90; Thomas F. Armstrong, "From Task Labor to Free Labor: The Transition Along Georgia's Rice Coast, 1820–1880," *Georgia Historical Quarterly*, LXIV (Winter, 1980), 432–33.

3. Clifton, "Half-Century," 391, 401–405; Clifton (ed.), *Life and Labor*, vii–xvii; Patience Pennington, *A Woman Rice Planter*, ed. Cornelius O. Cathey (Cambridge, Mass., 1961), xii–xvii; D. E. Huger Smith, *A Charlestonian's Recollections, 1846–1913* (Charleston, 1950), 56–57; George C. Rogers, Jr., *The History of Georgetown County, South Carolina* (Columbia, S.C., 1970), 252–324.

4. Joyner, "Slave Folklife," passim; Ira Berlin, "Time, Space, and the Evolution of Afro-American Society in British Mainland North America," *American Historical Review*, LXXXV (February, 1980), 61–65; *Compendium of the Tenth Census, 1880*, I, 340–42, 369; *House Reports*, 42nd Cong., 2nd Sess., No. 22 (Ku Klux Klan Hearings), Georgia, 305–306.

5. James B. Heyward to Louis Manigault, December 9, 1875, in Louis Manigault Papers, Perkins Library, Duke University; Clifton (ed.), *Life and Labor*, xxxv; Berlin, "Time, Space and the Evolution," 65–66; Gray, *History of Agriculture*, 551; Joyner, "Slave Folklife," 42–45, 229; Duncan Clinch Heyward, *Seed From Madagascar* (Chapel Hill, 1937), 183; Armstrong, "Task Labor to Free Labor," 434–36; Peter Wood, *Black Majority* (New York, 1974), Chap. 3.

6. Armstrong, "Task Labor to Free Labor," 437; Pennington, *Woman Rice Planter*, xii; J. H. Easterby (ed.), *The South Carolina Rice Plantation as Revealed in the Papers of Robert F. W. Allston* (Chicago, 1945), 206–13; Rogers, *History of Georgetown County*, 416–22; Nicholas B. Wainwright (ed.), *A Philadelphia Perspective: The Diary of Sidney George Fisher Covering The Years 1834–1871* (Philadelphia, 1967), 497–98; Page Smith, *Trial By Fire* (New York, 1982), 642.

7. "The Close of the War—the Negro, etc." (typescript copy of MS by Charles Manigault, South Caroliniana Library, University of South Carolina); Clifton, "Half-Century," 393–94, 409–11.

8. Easterby (ed.), *South Carolina Rice Plantation*, 211; Eric Foner, *Politics and Ideology in the Age of the Civil War* (New York, 1980), 132; Elias H. Deas to daughter, July 15, 1865, in Elias H. Deas Papers, South Caroliniana Library, University of South Carolina; Savannah Unit, Georgia Writers' Project, "Whitehall Plantation, Part III," *Georgia Historical Quarterly*, XXVI (June, 1942), 140; Daniel E. Huger Smith *et al.* (eds.), *Mason Smith Family Letters, 1860–1868* (Columbia, S.C., 1950), 236.

9. Rogers, *History of Georgetown County*, 428–34; Dorothy Sterling (ed.), *The Trouble They Seen* (Garden City, 1976), 39; Leon F. Litwack, *Been in the Storm So Long: The Aftermath of Slavery* (New York, 1979), 406–407; Myrta L. Avary, *Dixie After the War* (New York, 1906), 341; Savannah *Weekly Republican*, January 26, 1867; Savannah *Daily News and Herald*, January 21, 22, 23, 1867.

10. *Senate Executive Documents*, 39th Cong., 1st Sess., No. 27, p. 26; Heyward, *Seed From Madagascar*, 149–55; Edward B. Heyward to Allen C. Izard, July 16, 1866, Heyward to Katherine Heyward, n.d. [January, 1867], May 5, 1867, in Heyward Family Papers, South Caroliniana Library, University of South Carolina.

11. Smith *et al.* (eds.), *Mason Smith Letters*, 263–64; William B. Lees, "The Historical Development of Limerick Plantation, in Berkeley County, South Carolina, 1683–1945, a Tidewater Rice Plantation," *South Carolina Historical Magazine*, LXXXII (January, 1981), 44–62; Jacob Schirmer Diary, September 30, December 31, 1869, South Carolina Historical Society; Ben Allston to J. B. De Bow, September 14, 1866, in J. B. De Bow Papers, Perkins Library, Duke University; Easterby (ed.), *South Carolina Rice Plantation*, 18; Rogers, *History of Georgetown County*, 454–58; Frances Butler Leigh, *Ten Years on a Georgia Plantation Since the War* (London, 1883), 263–65; James M. Clifton, "Twilight Comes to the Rice Kingdom: Postbellum Rice Culture on the South Atlantic Coast," *Georgia Historical Quarterly*, LXII (Summer, 1978), 146–47; "Season of 1876," in "Statement of Sales, Gowrie Plantation, Savannah River," in Manigault Family Papers, Southern Historical Collection, University of North Carolina.

12. King, *Southern States of North America*, 436–37; Smith *et al.* (eds.), *Mason Smith Letters*, 230–31. For rice prices, see Jacob Schirmer Diary, December 31, 1870; Anne Bezanson, *Wholesale Prices in Philadelphia, 1852–1896* (Philadelphia, 1954), 273.

13. "Visit to Gowrie and East Hermitage Plantations," March 22, 1867, in "Statement of Sales, Gowrie Plantation, Savannah River," in Manigault Family Papers; Armstrong, "Task Labor to Free Labor," 442–43; David McPherson to Governor Daniel H. Chamberlain, June 30, 1876, in South Carolina Governor's Papers, South Carolina Archives; *New National Era*, September 25, 1873; Smith, *Charlestonian's Recollections*, 132.

14. Joel Williamson, *After Slavery: The Negro in South Carolina During Reconstruction, 1861–1877* (Chapel Hill, 1965), 135; A. M. McIver to Lt. J. M. Hoag, February 28, 1867, Unregistered Letters Received, ser. 1013, Savannah Sub-Assistant Commissioner, in Record Group 105, Freedmen's Bureau Papers, National Archives; *Address Delivered Before the Agricultural Society of South Carolina* (Charleston, 1872), 32.

15. *House Reports*, 42nd Cong., 2nd Sess., No. 22 (Ku Klux Klan

Hearings), Georgia, 305; Leigh, *Ten Years on a Georgia Plantation*, 55–56; Lt. Col. A. J. Willard to Bvt. Maj. H. W. Smith, December 6, 1865, Reports of Conditions and Operations, ser. 2929, South Carolina Assistant Commissioner, in Freedmen's Bureau Papers, NA.

16. J. R. Cheves to Maj. Gen. Davis Tillson, September 14, 1866, Unregistered Letters Received, ser. 632, Georgia Assistant Commissioner, Bvt. Lt. Col. B. F. Smith to Bvt. Maj. H. W. Smith, January 21, 1866, S–16 1866, Registered Letters Received, ser. 2929, South Carolina Assistant Commissioner, in Freedmen's Bureau Papers, NA; M. H. Wetson to Governor William W. Holden, October 16, 1868, in North Carolina Governor's Papers, North Carolina State Archives; William M. Hazzard to Governor Robert K. Scott, August 12, 1868, in South Carolina Governor's Papers; B. H. Pinner to Col. B. F. Smith, May 1, 1866, R. H. Nesbit to Col. B. F. Smith, April 20, 1866, Letters Received, ser. 2392, Post of Georgetown, in Record Group 393, Pt. 2, No. 142, NA.

17. Rogers, *History of Georgetown County*, 282, 425–31; Ralph I. Middleton to Henry A. Middleton, October 30, November 11, 1866, in Middleton Papers, Langdon Cheves Collection, South Carolina Historical Society.

18. Ralph I. Middleton to Henry A. Middleton, November 11, 1866, November 12, 1867, February 15, August 30, December 15, 1868, all in Middleton Papers, Langdon Cheves Collection.

19. Rogers, *History of Georgetown County*, 438, 444; Ralph I. Middleton to Henry A. Middleton, July 7, August 24, 1869, in Middleton Papers, Langdon Cheves Collection.

20. Ralph I. Middleton to Henry A. Middleton, August 24, 1869, Draft Agreement, Weehaw Plantation, January, 1870, Ralph I. Middleton to Henry A. Middleton, February 8, 1870, all in Middleton Papers, Langdon Cheves Collection.

21. Ralph I. Middleton to Henry A. Middleton, February 8, April 16, 1870, June 29, 1871, all in Middleton Papers, Langdon Cheves Collection.

22. Ralph I. Middleton to Henry A. Middleton, May 2, 1872, December 24, 1874, in Middleton Papers, Langdon Cheves Collection.

23. Charleston *News and Courier*, May 25, 1876; Smith, *Charlestonian's Recollections*, 126–27; James B. Heyward to Louis Manigault, October 11, 1876, in Louis Manigault Papers.

24. Smith, *Charlestonian's Recollections*, 131; A. W. Smith to Governor Robert K. Scott, June 24, 1872, in South Carolina Governor's Papers; King, *Southern States of North America*, 435–36; *House Miscellaneous Documents*, 44th Cong., 2nd Sess., No. 31, II, 85; C. J. Davis to Governor Daniel H. Chamberlain, March 6, 1876, David McPherson to Chamberlain, June 30, 1876, in South Carolina Governor's Papers. There is a detailed description of a visit to a large rice plantation owned by "Mr. B.," possibly Bissell, in *The Nation*, June 27, 1872, 418–19.

25. Thomas Holt, *Black Over White: Negro Political Leadership in*

South Carolina During Reconstruction (Urbana, 1977), 168; *Address Before Agricultural Society*, 32; Charleston *News and Courier*, May 25, 1876.

26. Charleston *News and Courier*, May 25, 29, 1876; John W. Burbridge to Governor Daniel H. Chamberlain, September 13, 1876, in South Carolina Governor's Papers; Holt, *Black Over White*, Appendix A.

27. Charleston *News and Courier*, May 24, 25, 27, 29, 1876.

28. Charleston *News and Courier*, May 24, 25, 1876.

29. H. H. Green to Governor Daniel H. Chamberlain, May 24, 1876, Ritcherson Green to Chamberlain, May 26, 1876, R. H. Colcock to Chamberlain, May 25, 30, 1876, all in South Carolina Governor's Papers; Charleston *News and Courier*, May 26, 1876.

30. Charleston *News and Courier*, May 23, 25, 27, 30, 1876; J. K. Terry to Governor Daniel H. Chamberlain, May 26, 1876, telegram, in South Carolina Governor's Papers; Holt, *Black Over White*, Appendix A.

31. Charleston *News and Courier*, May 29, September 6, 1876; Holt, *Black Over White*, 149, 215, Appendix A; Capt. James W. Grace to Governor Daniel H. Chamberlain, May 30, 1876, in South Carolina Governor's Papers.

32. Charleston *News and Courier*, May 31, 1876; David McPherson to Governor Daniel H. Chamberlain, June 30, 1876, John W. Burbridge to Chamberlain, September 13, 1876, in South Carolina Governor's Papers.

33. Charleston *News and Courier*, August 17, 1876.

34. Charleston *News and Courier*, August 23, 1876; Atlanta *Constitution*, August 26, 1876; H. M. Fuller to Governor Daniel H. Chamberlain, August 21, 1876, telegram, in South Carolina Governor's Papers; *Congressional Record*, 44th Cong., 2nd Sess., Appendix, 256.

35. Atlanta *Constitution*, August 26, 1876; Charleston *News and Courier*, August 25, 1876; Alfred B. Williams, *Hampton and His Red Shirts* (Charleston, 1935), 146–47; *Senate Miscellaneous Documents*, 44th Cong., 2nd Sess., No. 48, II, 401–405; William Elliott to Governor Daniel H. Chamberlain, September 12, 1876, in South Carolina Governor's Papers; *House Miscellaneous Documents*, 44th Cong., 2nd Sess., No. 31, II, 212.

36. *House Miscellaneous Documents*, 44th Cong., 2nd Sess., No. 31, II, 79–80; Savannah *Tribune*, September 2, 1876; Henry H. Fuller to Governor Daniel H. Chamberlain, August 23, 1876, telegram, Robert Smalls to Chamberlain, August 24, 1876, in South Carolina Governor's Papers.

37. King, *Southern States of North America*, 426–28; Edward B. Heyward to Katherine Heyward, n.d. [January, 1867], in Heyward Family Papers; Charleston *News and Courier*, August 24, 1876; B. F. Sellers to Governor Daniel H. Chamberlain, August 26, 1876, William Elliott to

Chamberlain, September 12, 1876, in South Carolina Governor's Papers.

38. *House Miscellaneous Documents*, 44th Cong., 2nd Sess., No. 31, II, 211; B. F. Sellers to Governor Daniel H. Chamberlain, August 26, September 1, 1876, in South Carolina Governor's Papers.

39. *House Miscellaneous Documents*, 44th Cong., 2nd Sess., No. 31, II, 66–68; Henry Taylor *et·al.*, to Governor Daniel H. Chamberlain, September 2, 1876, in South Carolina Governor's Papers; Charleston *News and Courier*, September 5, 6, 1876.

40. John W. Burbridge to Governor Daniel H. Chamberlain, September 13, 1876, James Low to Chamberlain, September 7, 1876, B. F. Sellers to Chamberlain, August 26, 1876, all in South Carolina Governor's Papers.

41. H. D. Warren to Governor Daniel H. Chamberlain, September 7, 1876, telegram, William Elliott to Chamberlain, September 12, 1876, John W. Burbridge to Chamberlain, September 13, 1876, all in South Carolina Governor's Papers; Charleston *News and Courier*, September 9, 1876; *House Miscellaneous Documents*, 44th Cong., 2nd Sess., No. 31, II, 210.

42. A. C. Shaffer to Governor Daniel H. Chamberlain, September 21, 1876, William Stone to Chamberlain, September 14, 1876, James Low to Chamberlain, September 14, 1876, all in South Carolina Governor's Papers; Beulah Glover, *Narratives of Colleton County* (n.p., n.d.), 126; Charleston *News and Courier*, September 13, 19, 1876.

43. Williams, *Hampton and His Red Shirts*, 188; *House Miscellaneous Documents*, 44th Cong., 2nd Sess., No. 31, II, 85–86, 89–96, III, 193–94.

44. [George C. Benham], *A Year of Wreck* (New York, 1880), 202; Chandra Jayawardena, *Conflict and Solidarity in a Guianese Plantation* (London, 1963), 57–58; Jayawardena, "Ideology and Conflict in Lower Class Communities," *Comparative Studies in Society and History*, X (July, 1968), 413–46; William Elliott to Governor Daniel H. Chamberlain, September 12, 1876, in South Carolina Governor's Papers.

45. *House Miscellaneous Documents*, 44th Cong., 2nd Sess., No. 31, II, 68–70; Williams, *Hampton and His Red Shirts*, 260–61, 328; Hampton M. Jarrell, *Wade Hampton and the Negro: The Road Not Taken* (Columbia, S.C., 1950), 71; Claude H. Nolen, *The Negro's Image in the South* (Lexington, 1967), 165.

46. "Statement of Sales, Gowrie Plantation, Savannah River," in Manigault Family Papers; James B. Heyward to Louis Manigault, May 27, July 5, 1876, in Louis Manigault Papers.

47. "List of Expenditures for Arms for Militia," October 9, 1873, Letters to Governor James M. Smith, August–September, 1876, Box 59, Capt. James T. Davis to Smith, August 31, 1876, all in Georgia Governor's Papers, Georgia Department of Archives and History.

48. "Statement of Sales, Gowrie Plantation, Savannah River," in

Manigault Family Papers; James B. Heyward to Louis Manigault, July 8, August 17, September 16, October 5, 11, November 3, 1876, E. H. Frost to Louis Manigault, December 6, 1876, all in Louis Manigault Papers; *House Miscellaneous Documents*, 44th Cong., 2nd Sess., No. 31, II, 86–88.

49. Charleston *News and Courier*, January 17, 1877; Holt, *Black Over White*, 167–69; Williams, *Hampton and His Red Shirts*, 395–96, 411.

50. George B. Tindall, *South Carolina Negroes, 1877–1900* (Columbia, S.C., 1952), 54–61; Philip S. Foner and Ronald L. Lewis (eds.), *The Black Worker During the Era of the Knights of Labor* (Philadelphia, 1978), 143–242, 367–404; Thomas W. Kremm and Diane Neal, "Challenge to Subordination: Organized Black Agricultural Protest in South Carolina, 1886–1895," *South Atlantic Quarterly*, LXXVII (Winter, 1978), 98–112; William F. Holmes, "The Demise of the Colored Farmers' Alliance," *Journal of Southern History*, XLI (May, 1975), 187–200.

51. Vernon L. Wharton, *The Negro in Mississippi, 1865–1890* (Chapel Hill, 1947), 121–22; D. Wyatt Aiken to Virginia S. Aiken, February 24, 1883, in D. Wyatt Aiken Papers, South Caroliniana Library, University of South Carolina.

52. Clifton, "Twilight Comes to the Rice Kingdom," 149–53; C. Vann Woodward, *Origins of the New South* (Baton Rouge, 1951), 119–20; G. W. McGinty, "Changes in Louisiana Agriculture, 1860–1880," *Louisiana Historical Quarterly*, XVIII (April 1935), 407–29; *Eleventh Census, 1890*, VI, 80, 426–27, 449; Rogers, *History of Georgetown County*, 488–89; Frederick C. Jaher, *The Urban Establishment* (Urbana, 1982), 399–401.

53. Ralph I. Middleton to Henry A. Middleton, April 20, 1877, in Middleton Papers, Langdon Cheves Collection. For examples of blacks acquiring land in the Upper South, see Robert F. Engs, *Freedom's First Generation: Black Hampton, Virginia, 1861–1890* (Philadelphia, 1979), 161–66; Richard P. Fuke, "Black Marylanders, 1864–1868," (Ph.D. dissertation, University of Chicago, 1973), 75–76; Sir George Campbell, *Black and White* (New York, 1879), 334, 345.

54. *Eleventh Census, 1890*, VI, 131–32, 178–79; Willie Lee Rose, *Rehearsal for Reconstruction: The Port Royal Experiment* (Indianapolis, 1964), 382; T. J. Woofter, Jr., *Black Yeomanry: Life on St. Helena Island* (New York, 1930), 140–45; Kay Young Day, "Kinship in a Changing Economy: A View from the Sea Islands," in *Holding on to the Land and the Lord*, ed. Robert L. Hall and Carol B. Stack (Athens, 1982), 12–13; William D. Armes (ed.), *The Autobiography of Joseph Le Conte* (New York, 1903), 234–35; *Report of the Committee of the Senate Upon the Relations Between Labor and Capital, and Testimony Taken by the Committee* (4 vols.; Washington, 1885), IV, 153, 234–35; Armstrong, "Task Labor to Free Labor," 443.

55. For recent definitions of the concept of peasantry, see Theodor Shanin, "Defining Peasants: Conceptualizations and Re-Conceptualizations Old and New in a Marxist Debate," *Peasant Studies*, VIII (Fall, 1979), 38–59; Martin A. Klein (ed.), *Peasants in Africa: Historical and Contemporary Perspectives* (Beverly Hills, 1980), 9–12. During the 1930s, Arthur F. Raper, in *Preface to Peasantry* (Chapel Hill, 1936), and other writers employed the concept with reference to southern blacks.

56. Thomas W. Simons, Jr., "A Century of Peasant Politics in East Central Europe," *Peasant Studies*, IV (April, 1975), 26–29.

57. Bureau of the Census, *Negro Population, 1790–1915* (Washington, 1918), 709–19, 744–45; Robert P. Brooks, *The Agrarian Revolution in Georgia, 1865–1912* (Madison, 1914), 110–14; Woofter, *Black Yeomanry*, 45, 117, 136–37; LaWanda Cox, *Lincoln and Black Freedom: A Study in Presidential Leadership* (Columbia, S.C., 1981), 221. A similar tendency to the subdivision of black holdings is noted in upcountry South Carolina in Elizabeth Bethel, *Promiseland: A Century of Life in a Negro Community* (Philadelphia, 1981), 62–64, 99–102.

58. Quoted in Perry Anderson, *Arguments Within English Marxism* (London, 1980), 17.

59. For coastal South Carolina today, see "Coastal Affairs," a special issue of *Southern Exposure*, X (May–June, 1982), esp. 33–39.

INDEX